The Writings of Joseph Sadony

"All mankind seems to have been seeking in the very air for something new to believe, something that will give them proof and understanding, something that will give their minds different food for thought, and of which they are now in greater need than food for the body."

       -- Joseph Sadony

REALFACE PRESS

Published by Realface Press
info@realface.com

ALSO PUBLISHED BY REALFACE PRESS

Holy Bible: King James Revealed Version,
translated by Bart Marshall

Becoming Vulnerable to Grace: Strategies for Self-Realization,
by Bart Marshall

*Christ Sutras: The Complete Sayings of Jesus
from All Sources Arranged into Sermons*,
compiled and composed by Bart Marshall

The Perennial Way, *Expanded Edition*,
translated by Bart Marshall

Bhagavad Gita: The Definitive Translation,
translated by Bart Marshall

The Emerald Tablets of Thoth the Atlantean,
edited by Bart Marshall

The Torah: The Five Books of Moses,
King James Revealed Version, translated by Bart Marshall

Ashtavakra Gita, translated by Bart Marshall

*Letters of Transmission: The Enlightenment Method of
Zen Master Alfred Pulyan*, edited by Bart Marshall

After the Absolute, by David Gold with Bart Marshall

The Conquest of Illusion, by J.J. van der Leeuw,
90th Anniversary Edition, edited by Bart Marshall

Verses Regarding True Nature, poems by Bart Marshall

Pearl of the Orient, a screenplay by Bart Marshall

Book of Psalms: A Psalter for Seekers in Extraordinary Times,
translated by Bart Marshall

The Triune Self: Confessions of a Ruthless Seer,
by Mike Snider

Table of Contents

Joseph Sadony

Editor's Preface

I was 22 years old in 1985 when I met Richard Rose, "The greatest man no one's ever heard of." Among so many other amazing characteristics, he was incredibly perceptive and intuitive. Shortly after I met him, while we were standing in a room full of people, he told me in his usual point-blank style that I was sensitive. Not in the emotional sense, but in the ability to directly apprehend — an intuitive feeling sense. I was completely oblivious to this innate tendency up until that point in my life. On that day, and for decades to come, Rose stirred in me an insatiable craving for a deeper understanding.

Joseph Sadony is the exemplar of the intuitive life. Two groups of readers will gravitate toward his writings. The first group are those who are fascinated by unusual mental abilities — "psychic phenomena," for lack of a better description. Sadony's startling experiences with intuition and his uncanny abilities are weaved throughout the book, and his stories are both compelling and convincing. The second group will ask, *"How?"* How did Sadony enlist such talents? How can I, the reader, improve my intuitive abilities and sensitivities to the "Great Broadcaster of Life," as he calls it?

Sadony admits that the *feeling* is a great mystery, and to explore it is the highest endeavor of humans. "It is the source of all inspiration, the fountainhead of all spiritual gifts, the heart and life of all religion." He fastidiously demystifies this feeling by refraining from labeling it as anything occult. Rather, he says, the feeling has neurological and physiological origins, not in the brain alone, but electrochemically through "the coordinated activity of the entire nervous organization." The feeler receives *something* through the nervous system and instantly pieces it together with previous memories and experiences. The feeler must suspend the intellect until after the feeling wraps itself in our imagination. Feeling shapes the thought.

Seekers of wisdom will quickly discover that aspiring to be a feeler means sensitizing the "mental clearinghouse" by remaining aware of the mind's activities. Intuition is alive when our mind is acting more like a receiver than a generator, and perhaps heightened further when body and mind are absorbed in creativity or exhausted with fatigue. We do not shape things. We allow the shape to form of its own accord and only then attempt to figure out what has been cast.

1

Above all, we must experience it for ourselves rather than rely on another's words.

What was Sadony's overall purpose for his prolific writings? He wanted to "rescue the truth," as he puts it, by exposing the charlatans and psychic racketeers who deceive us with tricks. He diligently demystified clairvoyance, extrasensory perception, precognition, telepathy, etc. by explaining and illustrating such phenomena in ordinary terms, and through personal examples in his life. Most of all, he wanted to show that inspiration and feeling compose the core of our heart, without which humanity would be but uninspired automatons with no purpose.

The Writings of Joseph Sadony is certain to enliven you.

Paul Constant

Gates of the Mind

The Proven Psychic Discoveries of Joseph Sadony

Foreword

No man can contribute to the world more than his own personal experience, the harvest of his own research and experiments, unless it be the fruit of inspiration or prophetic insight. The works of Joseph Sadony contain a rich store of both.

Though its subtitle is *Proven Psychic Discoveries*, various digressions from the narrative reveal that its purpose is not autobiographical. It is an introduction to the anatomy of prophetic intuition. The small book here privately printed is rather less than a "condensation." It contains but a small portion of the first volume of this unpublished work.

Underlying and eclipsing the narrative is a rationale of the physiological foundations and scientific investigation of mental phenomena considered as tele-empathic and telepathic phenomena of the human nervous system.

It is a conclusion of the author and his associates in research that most mystic, psychic, and occult terms used in describing mental phenomena are misleading, that there exist no mysterious "faculties" of a mystic or occult nature, but that the imagination, if used correctly, is capable of portraying past, present, or future events within the limitations imposed by the fact that the imagination is dependent entirely on memory of past sensory experience to provide the elements of its portrayal.

For example, the author claims that the term "thought-transference" is a misnomer, that it is impossible for what is usually designated a "thought" to be transferred from one mind to another mind, but that it is possible, and of common occurrence, to induce in another mind a thought that is similar to one experienced in your own mind, or *vice versa*. The exact degree of similarity will depend upon the similarity of past experience.

The induced thought, however, is entirely the product of the selective simulation of memory elements in an activity of the imagination. The thought is your own, and has not been "transferred" from another mind, even though it be similar in every respect. A phenomenon has taken place, but it is one of thought induction, not thought transference.

We are living through a crisis the full extent and meaning of which is realized by only a few. We are and have been witnessing periods of confusion and revolution, not only in world politics, in science, education, industry, and art, but also in psychology, philosophy, and religion.

We are witnessing, and shall witness, the collapse of theories and concepts in all fields of thought. No science can continue to stand on its present foundations without adjustments made necessary by the confusion and poverty of existing verbal organization. Neither the philosophies nor the psychologies can withstand the critical application of the operational view with any greater success than the physical sciences. They will be forced to a more strict correlation of *Language, Logic, and Life.*

Thus we have undergone, and are still undergoing, a revolution in the physical sciences. Even now, new foundations are being laid to complete the bridge extending from atomic to organic, thence to astronomic dimensions. The biologist must know his physics and chemistry as well as his psychology, and a psychologist without knowledge of the former is not worthy of the name. The philosopher who does not know by first-hand research and experimentation these fundamentals of life and the physical universe, must resign himself to his own amusement, for his mental structures can be only dialectic castles in the air.

The confusion of the age was manifest in the first few sessions of the Conference on Science, Philosophy and Religion at the opening of World War II. The scholars admitted that they were confused, and that they did not know how to "think with a view to action," or how to teach each other to the end of reaching mutual understanding and agreement. As a result they were forced to agree to disagree, to predict a pluralistic instead of a monolithic civilization.

Gates of the Mind is the beginning of an answer to the scholars on the part of a student of life and human nature, a seeker for truth and an independent investigator on an experimental basis of the operations of the human mind in relation to physiological and psychological consequences. Here for the first time is the beginning of a detailed account of a personal adventure in the deliberate and purposive development of prophetic intuition, and its application to problems of nature, human nature, science, philosophy, religion, education, industry, war and peace.

There has been the need for an effort on the part of someone capable of experiencing and demonstrating, as well as observing, so-called psychic and mental phenomena, to separate the wheat from the chaff, to paint the picture of just what can and cannot be expected of it in the present state of man's development, to differentiate the function of man's sympathetic sensitivities from all the technical and psychic "racketeering," to encourage the individual development of these sensitivities along healthy and constructive lines, and to discourage the authoritarian capitalization of psychological or spiritual truths and the subjugation of peoples by psychological tricks. In this small book is the beginning of Mr. Sadony's answer to this need.

And in answer to those who may ask, "Who is Joseph Sadony?" we quote data contained in *Who's Who in Michigan* and *Who's Who in the Central States*:

SADONY, Joseph A. Founder and director, Educational Research Laboratories, Montague, Michigan; columnist, Muskegon Chronicle (Mich.) since 1929 Home: "Valley of the Pines," Montague, Michigan; b. Montabaur, near Ems, Germany, Feb. 22, 1877; s. Alexander Nichols and Apollonia Reipert) S.; m. Mary Lillian Kochem, in 1906; ch. Joseph Jr. (1907), Arthur (1909). Came with parents to America in 1884 and located in Kalamazoo, Mich.; later moved to Chicago; traveled in West, walking eighteen hundred miles on foot investigating conditions in Indian Reservations for Theodore Roosevelt. In 1906 returned to Michigan and purchased 80-acre estate now known as the "Valley of the Pines" which he equipped with shops and laboratories later known as the Educational Research Laboratories, affiliated with Valley Research Corporation. Held office as constable, justice of the peace, spl. deputy sheriff, school moderator, dir. of the district school board, etc. Has done much good in his guidance and help to people and carries on an extensive correspondence throughout the world as "philosopher, guide and friend" (without compensation) to many thousands of people. For several years editor and publisher of *The Whisper* (an independent, international journalette of Prevenient Thought) and the "Voice of Tomorrow Calendar." Originator of "Plastic Prose" as a literary form adapted to radio script; author of *Fragments in Plastic Prose, My Answers*, and other works; technical papers: "Concerning Tidal Effects on Atmospheric Diathermancy," "The Function of Gravitation in the Determination of the Fundamental Constants and Ratios of the Physical Sciences," etc.; research developments and patents: moisture vapor barrier materials used by armed forces during the war; apparatus and methods of sonic

6

analysis for detection of defects in exhaust valves and other mental automotive parts. Member American Association for the Advancement of Science; Mason (past master, Montague Lodge No. 198 F. & A.M.); demit to Whitehall Lodge No. 310; Muskegon Commandery No. 22, Knight Templar, life member; served as organist for the Eastern Star (Mrs. Sadony being past worthy matron); Saladin Temple, AAONMS. Life member; De Witt Clinton Consistory, Grand Rapids.

From the view of some, a greater importance should be attached to the application of prophetic intuition to fundamental problems of science, philosophy, education, and religion, rather than to elements of mere personal experience. But to the laymen there can be nothing more important than how he can benefit by personal experience, rather than by the acquisition of knowledge or theory concerning the more abstruse problems of science or philosophy.

For his benefit, then, who cares little for the deeper problems that might be discussed at greater length, we may conclude this introduction by assuring him that so far as mental phenomena are concerned, together with the conclusions expressed in Mr. Sadony's comments in *Gates of the Mind*, we are only a few of many who will agree that they have been established with as much certainty for those of us who have participated in the experimental investigation of this subject, as have the results of our research in the fields of radionics, electrostatics, electro-magnetism, and gravitation.

Educational Research Laboratories

Introduction

It matters not who in the world of time the mind may be. Truth imprints upon its tablet its own law. If that mind is so constituted, it can no more help reflecting the fact than a mirror can help reflecting the rays of the sun if at just that angle to catch the eye as well as to send the reflection that will come to the human eye that receives it. The receiver is just as important as the sender.
—Joseph Sadony

Periodically in the history of the world it becomes essential for men mentally akin to find each other, to know each other, and in unison deliver a message of truth to enlighten, to strengthen, to correct mistakes, in an effort to avoid just what has happened to us all. But how is this to be done, if not by education? Not to condemn the methods of others, but to substitute a better way that will defend itself.

All religions embody good and have bettered the world. There are still two factors: Faith and Science—two rules, and both are evidently right. Is it expecting too much that Religion and Science together create the third principle, resulting in the transformation of the world into one human family of many children, each to his own? With Science to preserve order by eliminating fraud and trickery, there would be no fear of judging the innocent as guilty.

As man is inclined toward superstition, he naturally falls an easy prey to those clever enough to deceive his eye. In fact, some of the brightest minds of the nineteenth and twentieth centuries have been completely deceived in this way. The possibility of our loved ones returning after having passed away, or at least of sending us some message or thought, cannot be doubted. But it is the unreliability of the method used to receive these messages, as well as the unreliability of the person receiving them, that gives rise to a question. The truth is often exaggerated, and the open-minded victim easily duped.

Within mankind there is a power so great that it would be dangerous to know it until we are perfect in humility and self-control. Until then it is hidden from us by our selfish, animal nature, which causes the mind to become cloudy and discontented.

Even as trees sleep in the winter and blossom again in the spring, so also does humanity alternately sleep and blossom. Periodically come the fruits of genius, great minds and sensitive souls who give voice, as "human radios" to the great broadcasting of the ages, the Song of Truth. And with their passing, humanity gradually falls asleep again until the next "wave" or cycle.

In this spiritual sleep, this ebb of the soul, is the heyday of false prophets, and therein will be found the origin of superstition, in "imitation" of what did hold some truth, but is now a word without meaning, a body without a soul.

Why do supposedly great but false prophets and teachers flourish for a day and then die in obscurity, leaving no flourishing field to prove the fertility of their teaching?

The shell of the wheat was there, the words and phrases — all borrowed to feed people who do not think for themselves, and even when planted, gave up no fruit because the spirit of God was lacking, and because they who professed, denied the simplicity that is the soul itself.

Man slowly approaches the epoch of the human radio. His antenna of imagination opens that inner ear that hears the silent broadcast of the ages. It still vibrates in the atmosphere. Man's mortal ear already hears the music and the words...

We may view this psychologically rather than from a spiritual or religious point of view. Nevertheless, it is clear that an even greater revelation will accompany the discovery of a "radio" in the human mind than what took place industrially, internationally, and domestically with the invention and introduction of radio into our homes.

The entire universe is within the human head in the same manner that music broadcast from various cities all over the world is within the radio, or within the room in which it is being received. We forget that a well-governed and trustworthy imagination contains the tools that make education from the specifications of wisdom, that therein also are the antennae of man with which he searches for God — that aerial to receive the message, the chamber of transformation in which the "word is made flesh," where thoughts are dramatized in symbols that are revelations if they be attuned to "facts."

We still have more to learn of the rooms of man's mind, to find the doors leading to that religious ecstasy, the mystery, the frenzy of the aborigines, the bliss of divinity felt by martyrs and saints, the hypnotic power of our professional men — all still in its infancy.

No one will deny facts, unless he has a subtle purpose to use opportunities for selfish purposes. Truth is self-evident and needs no support. It supports itself. And if the pillars of a structure are lies, it will collapse. Still, the spirit of true support is ever present, so that a

9

new permanent structure shall rise from the ashes and dust of falsehood. There are ever-present health germs to continue life, even among death germs. That is the law of adjustment, compensation and growth — the manifestation of life.

All that matters most to man is in behind his own eyes, and there he flounders in the dark, thinking he thinks a thought, but unaware of the origin of that thought, or of its fruits — "imagining" things without the slightest conception of the power and mechanism he is using.

Surely, we may learn much by watching the insect with its antennae moving in every direction, sensing the danger we cannot see. It protects itself without the great gift to man: Imagination. It only acts upon its inherent power of instinct. It uses its antennae to sense approaching danger, which it avoids, but knows not its source, without reason. Why should not man have a more highly developed sense by the protection of reason, or the cause with its effect?

If the same amount of energy and education had been utilized for psychological, mental, and spiritual power as for the comforts of economic, mechanical, and electrical power, what would have been accomplished to further the progress of humanity? There is no excuse for man to underestimate the power of the mind at the loss of his inheritance from God or Nature, from ancestry, or self-acquired. If we refuse to use reason and logic as a foundation to intuition, whom can we blame for the failure in evolution? Whom but our own negligence? Nature offers us her fruits. Why are men ashamed to admit their belief for or against spirituality?

How can anyone judge or give an opinion of the power of prayer, of Christianity, or of the prophets, unless he has given it a lifetime of experience to see the answer, and then left us the records, by which we may judge?

There is much that might be said of certain facts and truths that would but compel us to search the Book of Mistakes made by those who were sincere, but too enthusiastic to allow Nature to grow in its own good time — where swords have been unsheathed without provocation, only in fear of apparently losing opportunities. If there be any loss, let us go back and see whether the purse had a hole in it, whether the compass was influenced by a nail, whether the watch kept good time as it should, or whether we were controlled by our stomach, our heart, or our mind...

We are ever traveling toward the future, where all truth is born. Should we waste time in disputing the possibility of truth we think we have not, or be open to the possibilities that the world shall know tomorrow, as yesterday gave us for today?

We have a duty we owe to humanity — to those who have knocked upon doors of empty churches, temples, and schools, but not prisons. We must help men and women who can do work, not as missionaries, nor under the flags of politics, cults, or -isms, but just pure, clean-hearted leaders who are handicapped, discouraged and held back, who are being used as steppingstones to respectability by the profane.

Why waste time, paper, and ink analyzing flavors, the taste of fruit? Let us eat what Nature has given for thousands of years, and turn it into good health, joy, long life, and normal appreciative thoughts, so that the real knowledge of life may be born normally for today and tomorrow, and not for thousands of years hence.

We cannot afford to spend much time considering the opinions or methods of yesterday, nor stop to harvest their fruits today, when we must plant for a new generation, knowing that all those who do not now understand, will gradually do so as time passes, for "Time proveth all things."

The individual awakening and cultivation of intuition is the foremost concern of all leaders and teachers who may be pioneering in the prevenience of a new era. Until all education is "prevenient education," our problems as a nation shall not be solved.

Written history contains no records of a nation in the position in which the United States of American now stands, with the possibilities in its hands for the manifestation of a spirit of prevenience that would enable it to become the dominating culture of a new epoch by demonstrating a new level of revolutionary "warfare" without muscle and bloodshed, as an example to set before the other nations of the world.

Who shall plant the seeds of the new viewpoint in the ground thus made ready? Who but those thinkers and leaders who prove by their stability, adaptability, reliability, and endurance that they have been chosen by their own fertility to survive as the foundations for new structures and the roots of a new generation?

As Americans, should we not fight for what America represents, as the melting pot of the world, with many laws inherited, yet obeying but one law, that of our pioneering forefathers for freedom of thought, speech, and religion founded on logic, reason, and reality, as well as (and above all) one Supreme Being of power that may be clothed in any raiment desired, but internally one and the same hub of that *Wheel of Truth*, where the spokes are teachers and exemplifiers, and the rim, those whose personal responsibility is to protect those who teach, and the steel hoop, the beasts of burden, and the movements, the combined machinery of the world?

Things have only been partly done. The mansion is still in process. We are all but workers at the scaffolding (parties and divisions) of America as well as Christianity. When a mansion is done, what happens to the scaffolding? It is torn down, revealing the completed examples as models for a Universal Christianity and a United Nations of the World.

The two are inseparables, the north and south poles of each other, the spirit and the body, the ideals and the nation, the way of life and the government to make it possible. Can we expect to crystallize Utopia and usher in the long-heralded *Millennium*? That's not the question. It is the dream and the vision that point down the highway. Though we fall by the wayside and never reach it, we must believe in it. Otherwise we travel in a vicious circle. It is only the hope that leads us on.

The problems of the ages still face us, but today we are better equipped than ever before to understand them, if we will only discard the limiting thought habits of ancestral education, and adopt the mental tools and implements offered us today, with which to understand and shape tomorrow.

What excuse have we to neglect a progress that we may further in our own way? Who should be to blame in the misunderstanding of a bugle call—the wounded lips that fail to shape the notes, the bugle, or the man who is supposed to know the signal and fails to execute it?

Someone must hit the gong so the blind may hear the hour. Another must turn the hands for the deaf, so they may see. Why the slate and chalk, memory's purpose and traces of the blueprint? Surely there must be many laborers to one architect or overseer. Why should we deny our destiny? If there be an effect, surely there has been a cause. If we hear an echo there must have been a voice to send it. If you or I have an ideal to express, whence came its cause? Others may try to play music and fail. Why? Is it for the want of a piano, a melody, or trained fingers?

If you have dreams and visions only, without framing them exposed to eyes that seek them, you speak a language that you alone understand. It is useless to those called to cooperate with you— workmen of the temple idle, waiting for your designs while you sleep, and they vanish. Whom do you think shall spin, weave, work in the quarries, or gather timber to materialize dreams given you, if you fail to sing your melody?

Why cannot more men utilize the gifts they really possess, but which they do not seem to realize are in their possession? Why carry the newly felled trees to be made into lumber, when beasts of burden would gladly carry them for a cast-off meal? Why all the spiritual confusion throughout the world, when there is no discord where truth exists?

How many fine minds are there hidden in obscurity at the front line of commercialism, shackled to an organization because of wages and an inferiority complex, while if but allowed to dream — away from the grinding note of gears — a new musician, poet, or scientist may be born. Give men a chance to spread their shallow or clay roots. The top can always be pruned from faults. But let their roots alone, to allow character to prove their value before we forget why we live, and how.

Why do not men of learning come together to exchange views, as pugilists do blows, wrestlers, holds, athletes, feats of endurance, so that monuments of knowledge may be like large, fine trees as landmarks to the wayfaring man who is traveling through unknown lands, the labyrinth of the world's paths, to his home and loved one, whether mortal or immortal, and do those things of the sake of truth instead of wealth and glory? Truth itself is glorified, and so are they who dispense it.

The progress of the world's education, research, and understanding would be so much more enhanced if we allowed thinking men to do their thinking without a handicap. Let them be able to think and do their best while the man with muscle removes stumbling blocks so the dreamer may dream visions governed by thinkers for the doers to give it life.

If each man or personality in the entire world represented an individual key to his greatest treasure vault, we would not need to fear a burglar picking our lock, for no two keys would be alike. Still, all are expected to eat from the same plate the same amount, dress alike, be punished alike, be rewarded alike, and die alike. Why not examine the tumblers of these human locks and see who should be trusted most, and with what responsibility, so that we will find geniuses to teach us short methods, instead of waiting for them every century or so?

The trouble with most of us is that we shape things to suit ourselves, according to past acquirements, whereas we should permit truth to come to us, crystallizing in its own shape, then try to figure out what the shape is.

13

The seed of truth must preserve itself for future generations in a vocabulary untainted by those words that have attracted to themselves all the odium of a confusion of fraudulence, fakery, trickery, and overgrown superstition. The world is waiting for someone to come to teach them, all looking in different directions for another coming, save those who believe that He has already come.

Does one appear upon a crest of notoriety? Then it is not He. Did he found a cult or a "system"? The Maser himself comes not in these ways—but as a breeze across a prairie where labor all notions, all races, sects, and creeds…each fanned by the breeze, and differently, each giving expression to his reception and appreciation of the One Gentle Breeze through this world, each clothing a Christ in virtues thus conceived.

One is wet, and the breeze dries him. One is covered with dust, and it blows away this dust, fanning the hair from his eyes. One draws a bow at his enemy, and the breeze prevents, carrying it back to the sender. One aims with the breeze a dart just to warn, and fall short of its mark, but the breeze carries it on to the heart of him who deserved the death-blow that it was…

At best we are but cogs in the Wheel of Time, and call it "history," which is but the echo for philosophers, the flames and smoke rolling away, cause and effect blinded by the blindness of man to know neither the beginning nor the end, nor what is one— thinking mortal what is immortal, feeling the heat, seeing the smoke, combining nothing as one cause, thinking only in jets, as the beating and breathing of heart and lungs. Is it not true?

The only cause a man has for not realizing his power as a man, is that he never has tried to select the mental food his brain should digest to prove how in all simplicity his ideals lie at his feet, if he will but select the mental food to accomplish all his desires that but cast their shadow before him. Let him but awaken his gift of logic and reason to realize that to think a thing is to shape action, energy, and influence to that creation thought. For we only want those things made manifest by what we have allowed our brain to consume.

Thus we arrive at the purpose of these prefatory and fragmentary paragraphs, which is to provide a few samples of the food for thought that has sustained me in the continuation of that quest of which the beginning is subjected to both chronicle and commentary in *Gates of the Mind*.

Joseph Sadony, Valley of the Pines, January, 1948

Chapter 1

We are not so alone today [1948] as we were forty-five years ago. Turn on your radio and see. And what will you say within forty-five years more? May you not then hear the whispering thoughts of loved ones gone before you within their past silence, as it was half a century before — only waiting for us to find the spiritual dial, as we found the material one, within the mind and hand of man who did seek, and who found it — but shadow of the real yet to come?
— Joseph Sadony

My mother was showing me a picture. She said, "That is where I was born, Joseph." For a minute I looked at it, and it didn't seem right.

I said, "But Mother, shouldn't there be a river over here?" I pointed to the right. "And shouldn't there be a barn besides just a house?"

"What makes you say that, Joey? The artist made this just like it was. No, we were away from the river. We had no barn. What makes you say that?"

"Well, anyway," I said, "I remember the river, and a barn and a bridge."

Mother said, "Joseph, you mustn't talk like that. You never went as far as the river. You couldn't possibly remember it. Besides, that's where your father was born. It was his father who had a — "

Suddenly, my mother stopped and looked at me biting her lower lip. For a moment she seemed not to see me, though looking right at me.

I said, "Mother! What's the matter?"

She said, "Joseph, you couldn't possibly remember that, because you were never there, but that's where your father was born, by the river, near a bridge. And your grandfather had a barn, because he had horses. That was on the Rhine, near Coblens."

Herman was my only brother, and he was older than I was. When I was seven, he was twelve. He was a cripple from birth, but he was beautiful and he was good. I always went to Herman when I didn't understand something and no one else would talk with me.

It was spring, and we were watching a robin build a nest outside the window. I said, "Do you think that's the same one that built there last year, the nest that fell down when the wind blew this winter?"

15

Herman said, "I think it's maybe one of the young ones that was born in the old nest."

I said, "But how would it know? If it was born in the old nest, how would it know how to build a new one? Can a mother robin teach it?"

???

"But how?" I insisted.

"Well, they call it instinct, Joey, but what that is I can't tell you. I guess it's born in them because the mother and father knew, back and back so far nobody knows anything about it."

"Herman, do you think we know things because Mother and Father knew them, even if they don't tell us?"

"Well, I think maybe we feel things and do things like they did, Joey. I've heard Father say you are sometimes just like Grandpa Jean Marie Felix Reipert. He was a bookbinder, like Uncle, and an artist too, always working with his hands, making things like you do."

I said, "Herman, sometimes I feel as if I could almost remember things before I was born. But just when I think I do, I forget it again. Do you ever feel that way?"

Herman said, "Well, I know what you mean. It's like a dream. When you wake up you can't remember it, but you know you were dreaming."

I said, "Yes, only it's not when I'm asleep, Herman. It's when I'm awake, and when I've been thinking and then stop thinking for a minute. When I start thinking again, it's gone."

Herman looked at me a minute and said, "You've always been funny that way, Joey. When you say things without thinking you are usually right, and everyone wonders how you know. But when you think about things you act as if you didn't know anything at all. I suppose you know that sometimes worries Mother, because she's afraid Father won't understand it. He doesn't like that sort of thing one little bit."

"But what can I do about it, Herman?"

"Well, I wouldn't say too much without thinking when Father is around. It's better when he thinks you're dumb than when he worries, wondering what's got into you. Someday I'll tell you why he worries about it."

"Tell me, Herman! Please tell me!"

"Ssh! Joey, they'll hear us. I'll tell you sometime when nobody's home but you and me."

It was pitch dark and I woke from a nightmare in a cold sweat. I must have cried out in my sleep because Mother had her hand over my mouth, whispering, "Be quiet, Joseph! Don't wake your father. What were you dreaming?"

I said, "I dreamed that Herman was hanging on the wall with his arms out, like on a cross. He was nailed there."

My mother gasped and said, "Joey! Promise me you won't tell anyone that! Don't tell your father, and don't tell Herman or your sisters."

I promised, and then asked, "Why?"

"Because," she said, "your father doesn't like such things, and we mustn't think of them or tell about them. But you frighten me."

"I'm sorry, Mother."

"I'm not blaming you, Joseph. You can't help how strange it is. I dreamed a dream like that about Herman the night you were born, and I didn't dare say anything about it. Because eight months before you were born I started dreaming strange dreams, and they all came true. That never happened to me before, and it has never happened since you were born. But during that time all my dreams came true except that last one about Herman. You're the first I've told, because now you dream it too! Let us say a prayer, Joey, and not tell anyone."

So Mother left me, but I didn't sleep. Something troubled me, but I did not know what it was. It was something more than my dream about Herman, something that made me feel all alone in the world, even with a large family.

I lay in the dark, then suddenly something happened to me that I did not comprehend until years later, in memory. The vague distress of an internal conflict I could not understand suddenly vanished. In that moment I gained a new sense of identity. Yet I felt like a stranger in the bosom of my own family. Suddenly, I didn't know who I was, and lay there in the dark asking myself, "Who am I? Where am I? How did I get here?"

But there was no uneasiness in the sensation. Rather, a sense of impending excitement, as if I had entered a new world and could hardly wait to explore it. Somewhere in this new world a treasure was hidden, and I would find it. For some reason my heart was glowing as if I had fallen in love with something I couldn't see. All my inner senses were affected by this, so that strong, tender arms picked me up, but I could see no face because I was suddenly tired, and suddenly safe. When I awoke, it was morning.

The world was the same, after all, but something inside of me was different. I felt happy about something and didn't know why. I saw more than I usually did. I stopped to look at things that I usually passed by, and when I looked at the same old things I had seen every day, I now saw something I hadn't before, and identified them in my mind. I heard sounds and knew what they meant without turning my head to look. I felt the urge to go out exploring, but suddenly felt the need of sharing all this new world with someone who would understand it. I thought of Herman, but he was crippled and couldn't go with me.

So I stayed home with Herman. I couldn't tell him about my dream, so I asked him, "Herman, can't you tell me now why Father worries about what gets into me? Mother is outside now. No one will hear us. The girls have gone too. What is Father worried about? What does he think is going to happen to me?"

"Well, he thinks something gets into you, Joey. And he doesn't know whether it's a devil or an angel. Sometimes he's sure it's a devil, and that it'll lead you to no good end. Remember how one time you would run off with his gun and go shooting by the castle on the Rhine, and next thing he knew you would be playing priest with an old soap box for an altar, serving mass? One day you would be catching crabs down by the pond, and spend hours looking at the worms you would break out of those long stick-like things you found. And next day you would imitate Saint Joseph, and say you wanted to be a carpenter."

"Do I have to be the same all the time, Herman?"

"Not for my part, Joey. That's what I like about you. One never knows what you are going to say or do next."

"Doesn't Father like that?"

"Well, it isn't just that. It's when you say things about the future, or when you seem so positive about something you couldn't possibly know. And when things happen to you that are mysterious."

"But nothing mysterious happens to me, Herman."

"Do you remember the time you had Uncle take you coasting on Montabaur hill? You didn't have a sled, so you took a ladder instead. The hill was all ice, and at the bottom was the crossroad. Uncle said a team of horses was coming, but it was too late for him to stop you, and you could not stop yourself. He said there was nothing on earth could keep you from being killed or badly hurt."

"But I wasn't hurt a bit, Herman."

"That's just the thing, Joey. Ladder and all, you shot right through between the legs of the horses, entirely unhurt. How did you do it? You didn't know. No one knew. That was a mystery. And then when they asked you if you weren't frightened when you saw the team ahead of you, you said no, you weren't, because the minute you saw them you thought about something else and forgot all about them."

"Well, I did, Herman, I closed my eyes, and saw the picture in the church."

"Yes, I know, Joey. But you said you knew you weren't going to be hurt."

"I did know it. I wasn't hurt."

"Well, all right. I believe you. But I'm showing you what worries Father. When they asked you how you knew you weren't going to be hurt bad or killed, you said it was because you were going to marry a girl named Mary, with black eyes and dark hair when you were twenty-seven years old, so that's how you knew you weren't going to be killed before then."

"That's how I did know, Herman."

"Well, that's what Father doesn't like. It's either nonsense, or you know. And if you know, how do you know? He doesn't like it either way, Joey."

So that night I lay there again in the dark feeling like a stranger, I tried to remember how it all came about that I was there, and why I felt like I sometimes did. It was the "feeling" that made me say things and think things like Herman said Father didn't like, and Mother seemed to understand but hushed me up so he wouldn't hear me.

I was six years old we were still in Montabaur, when there began to be talk in the family about going to America. It was then that I began to be conscious of a world beyond the village limits. I climbed to the top of the hill to try to see some of it. I was alone, but I imagined that men were walking up the hill with me, and that I was one of them.

We all had on light, flexible suits of armor, like fish scales made of metal. There was a bright red cross on each breast, a sword in one hand and a Bible in the other.

It was fifty years before I found out, inadvertently, that the village of Montabaur and the hill I climbed that day were originally called Humbach, and that centuries before me the Crusaders had climbed that hill and looked down over the beautiful country, calling it "The Holy Land." The hill reminded them of that Mount that Christ had ascended to pray, with Peter, James and John, where He was transfigured before them. So they christened it Mount Tabor, and henceforth the little village at its foot was called Montabaur.

19

I did not know this as I trudged along that day, surrounded by the creation of my own imagination, a company of Christian warriors with swords and Bibles.

When I reached the top I still could not see America. So I closed my eyes, but all I could "see" was a lot of Indians. That was of course because of what I had heard about America.

So far as I know now I had no knowledge of the Crusaders, or in any case of their relation to the hill at Montabaur. Of course it is possible there was a foundation for the "image play" with my remembering it. The fact is here unimportant as the purpose of these early recollections is more to provide the background and to portray the general nature of early thought elements as based on experience.

At present this is merely illustrative of a later problem: *What distinguishes a "true" imagination from a "false" one* as an element of imaginative experience when it is regarded as an established fact that *we can think only with what we have acquired to think with?* In other words, all imaginative experience is made up of combinations and recombinations of elements of sensory experience with a physiological foundation. Nevertheless, it has been established by experiment that the separate parts or memory elements may be put together correctly or incorrectly to form a true or false internal representation of external events or conditions. What distinguishes between the "true" and the "false" when immediate verification by observation or experiment is impossible?

The answer, later to be set forth more fully, is that the distinguishing characteristic of a "true" imagination is a "feeling" that must be felt in order to understand its nature.

I did not at first comprehend this, but now in looking back at many thousands of imaginative experiences of childhood and youth, I see that when the exercise of the imagination is either unaccompanied by any feeling whatsoever, or when the imagination produces a feeling as a result of its exercise (e.g. imagining Indians is followed by a feeling of excitement and anticipation), the imagination is not to be trusted unless a train of thought is followed back to determine its origin, and unless the logic and reason are sufficiently matured and trained to adjust and retouch the picture in accordance with experience, or reason based on observation and experiment.

On the other hand, if a certain type of "feeling" (which is a dominant experience throughout this record) precedes the exercise of the imagination, and in fact produces the imagination by selective stimulation and blending of memory elements to express, to clothe, to

20

embody, or to interpret the "feeling," we have then a type of spiritual inspiration and mental phenomena that merits further investigation, to which an introduction will be found in these pages.

My first experiences of a distinction in feeling associated with imagination were largely unrealized at the time, but preserved in memory. In climbing Mount Tabor, for example, the "feeling" came over me first that I was not alone. This caused me to imagine myself surrounded with companions all starting out together for some distant place to fight a battle. We would have swords but we would also have Bibles. The Cross would be our armor inside, but outside we would need armor of steel.

I did not then realize that these details characterized the Crusaders, who gave the hill historic background and a name. All the elements were familiar to me, but not the history. My memory contained swords, Bibles, Crosses, metal armor, and the idea of men who would use these things. Emphatically, I did not see the "spirits" of Crusaders walking up the hill with me. What I "saw" was entirely the product of my own imagination in which was composited various elements of memory acquired by previous sensory experience.

But these memory elements were selectively stimulated, assembled, and imbued with life by a "feeling" at a particular time, under a particular condition, at a particular place, which invested them with a meaning I did not myself comprehend until fifty years later. *Whence and what the "feeling"?* Why the particular mental imagery evoked by the feeling? Not in these few childhood cases alone, but in thousands upon thousands of cases extending through a lifetime—my own and the lives of many others whose experiences I have investigated.

That was the quest in which, symbolically at least, I set forth with a sword in one hand and a Bible in the other, to find the answer. I sought the truth, and as time went on, I found that my imagination provided the truth in one instance and deceived me in another. It deceived me when I used my own reason and memory to speculate on things I didn't know enough about. It deceived me when I concentrated or "tried." It never deceived me when I didn't try, and didn't care, and had a "feeling" first that started my imagination going to piece together in a flash what was aroused from my memory by the feeling. *What was the feeling?*

I stress this because as time went on, people who knew more about such things than I would say, "The boy is psychic," or, "He is clairvoyant." "It must be telepathy or psychometry," and so on.

21

And I knew they were all wrong. I possess no special, mystic, or occult sense that other men do not possess. My mental operations are limited entirely to what I have acquired and recorded by sensory experience. My imagination has only my own memory to draw on. I visualize something spontaneously past, present or future, near or far; it proves correct, with witnesses to verify it. My records contain thousands of such witnessed cases in which I was correct 98% of the time. What did I "see"? Nothing but a composite of my own memory elements of past experience.

Truly and literally it was "nothing but my imagination." Still it corresponded with the truth. *Why?* Was it a good guess? Was it "coincidence"? Was it "chance"? These were questions to be answered by experimental research. At first, I did not know. But time ruled out chance beyond all dispute. And I did soon find out that man's most important thinking does not take place in the brain alone, but with the entire body and nervous system.

Truth is not to be found in man's memory of words or his reflective visual or oral thinking. Words and memories of sights and sounds may be woven together into endless combinations. *What gives them meaning?* What determines the exact word or memory elements that will be combined in any given concept or idea or train of thought? What assurances have we that our ideas have any correspondence with reality at all?

Our only assurance from a scientific point of view is one based on experience, observation and experiment. How then is it possible to know things in the future, at a distance in the present and in the past, without opportunity for experience, observation, or experiment? I can only say that I have established this fact for myself, that I am writing this commentary on my early experience to introduce you to what I did and how I did it, so you too may establish the facts for yourself, without taking anyone's word for it—mine or that of anyone else.

It requires not the use of some mysterious faculty you do not possess, but rather the suspension of the use of your "intellect" (verbal memory, reason, etc.) until after your feeling of intuition has clothed itself imaginatively. Then harness it by "logic and reason," by all means, if you can. But you must first learn how to stop thinking at will. You must learn how to "deconcentrate" instead of concentrating. You must make no strenuous "effort." You can't "force" it. You can't "play" with it. You can't "practice" it. Spontaneity is its most essential characteristic. It cannot manifest in the realm of habit or "conditioned reflexes," as in the case of instinct.

In the language of the New Testament, you must not try to move the spirit, you must let the spirit move you. This means that you must let the truth shape you, for the simple reason that you cannot shape the truth. Your relation to truth is direct, and not by reflective or verbal representation. You will find the truth neither in words nor in memories, but only in direct nervous coordination of the whole of your immediate sensory experience, internal as well as external.

Just as the law of crystallization and chemical combination in the mineral kingdom and the inorganic world, so also the law of selective absorption in the organic world and vegetable kingdom, preserving the species, materializing the truth and meaning of the seed. And so also the selective excitation and conditioning of reflexes in the formation and operation of instinct in the animal kingdom. And there is evidence that a similar law is at work in a more complicated system of self-conditioning reflexes, as manifest in the vastly superior nervous organization of man — a mechanism of adaptation not only to so-called seen or visible environments, but also to "unseen" environments, such as those manifest in radiant energy and the specifications of future growth, as manifest in seeds.

All I knew as a child was that I had some sort of relation with what I could neither see, hear, smell, taste nor touch, and that relation was a "feeling."

But I found that "thinking" and "imagining" first created a false feeling that lied to me. It was only when the feeling came first, without thinking, that the feeling was right. And my thoughts and imaginations were right only if they were induced by the feeling, and not by association of thought resulting from what I saw or heard. Sometimes there was nothing in my experience to fit the feelings that came to me. Often, I could not understand them at all in terms of word or ideas familiar to me. Still I "knew," but I could not explain it.

I feel it necessary, for the sake of the intellect of those who have had no such experiences, to explain at length the view from which my own are regarded. None was regarded as occult or mystic in nature. None involved mysterious unknown senses, nor were they "extra-sensory" or "super-sensory." Man's relation with his environments, the universe, the rest of mankind, Deity, or forms of energy or life beyond his present understanding is regarded as a physiological, neurological, sensory relation. No responsive or imaginative activity is regarded as possible without a nervous organization with a physiological foundation. And I have established to my own satisfaction by experiment that if I apparently "see" a vision or dream,

23

a dream that proves to be prophetic, there is no so-called faculty of prevision, or second sight. The "third eye" employed in such experiences is nothing more nor less than the "imagination" that every man, woman, and child exercises to a greater or lesser degree. This "mind's eye" of imagination has never, does not, cannot, and never will "see" anything outside of one's own physiological organization. Its sensations are entirely "memory sensations." It is strictly limited to the momentary and fragmentary revival of past experiences as recorded in memory. Its one and essential power, which distinguishes the complicated nervous organization of man from the simpler one of the animal, is the power of recombination by means of which the imagination can make new creations out of the memory elements of old experiences.

Thus we symbolize, indulge in fantasy, speculate and theorize, create works of art, invent—and thus we produce a culture and a civilization. But as we thus change environments, we change our "destiny," and we change the character of adaptation that operates in the law of the survival of the fit. It becomes necessary to adapt oneself to subtler and more complicated environments. It becomes necessary to develop foresight, a knowledge of consequences—to plan, to prepare, to prevent. We find that only those who do this, survive.

So now we have a law of the survival of the intuitively fit. But *intuition* needs to be redefined, or we shall have to find a new word for it.

Possibly there was a time when brute strength survived, but it soon became evident that a less strong and more sensitive nervous organism better adapted itself to environments in the survival of the instinctively fit.

With the appearance of man there was a new element: Intelligence. Neither brute strength nor instinct could cope with it. The intellect that could make a trap, dig a pitfall for mastodons, and invent a gun soon became king of the earth.

And then what, as men fight each other as well as the elements of nature, to say nothing of man's own creations, which break his bones and blast him from the face of the earth? Do the strong battle and kill themselves off so that the meek shall inherit the earth?

Man now finds others than himself to battle. He builds cities, and the earth trembles, opens great jaws and swallows them up. Volcanoes belch forth and bury them. Winds blow and lay them low. The rain falls and great floods sweep all before them. Lightning strikes and burns his structures to the ground. He builds ships and they sink

24

at sea. He makes fast-moving engines and dashes to destruction. He digs in the bowels of the earth for its riches and is buried alive. The sun dries up his crops and he perishes in famine. Pestilence breaks out and leaves a city of dead to be buried unknown by the sands of ten thousand years, which he later digs up to decipher its records. And ever and anon, as the beating pulse of an eternal war drum, he goes to battle again, with ever increasing cunning in horrible devices with which to slay — *himself.*

It is the last cycle, the final "survival." And is it the strong who survive? Is it the cunning? Is it the meek? Is it the tyrant? Is it the selfish and arrogant? It is not. It is they who feel the "feeling" and act on it. It is they who had a "hunch" not to buy tickets on the ship that was going to sink. It is they who did not build a city where Vesuvius would belch forth its lava and flames. It is they who do not buy or build a house below the future flood-crest of a river. It is they who packed their belongings and left the day before an earthquake shattered their home. It is they who do these things without even thinking why.

What is the "feeling"? If we waited to use it until we knew what it was, we would be like the farmer who still uses kerosene lamps because he doesn't intend to use electricity until he knows what it is. The wren does not know why it flies south, but it flies, and thus escapes cold and starvation. An animal obeys a "feeling" directly, without translating it into words or thoughts of visual (imaginative) representation. Man has so far lost his neural relation with reality (by having substituted a world of words and symbolic representations) that he regards as abnormal those who retain it or regain it. He invests it with an air of mystery, and represents it by misleading words of special vocabularies — mystic, occult, theosophical, theological, psychological and psychic.

The mystery is no longer in the physiological and nervous organization of man — not any more than in the construction of the Geiger counter. The mystery is in the so-called cosmic rays that act on the Geiger counter. What are they, and where are they from? The mystery is in the source of energy or life that acts on the nervous organization of man to produce the *feeling.* What is it, and where is it from? There need be no other mystery.

The organism upon which it acts is now fairly well known. New ductless glands will be discovered. Many functions and operations will be better understood. But in all its essentials the physiological foundation and nervous organization is well enough understood, in the light of developments in the field of electronics and

25

radiant energy, to know that man is capable of experiencing "feelings" (independent of seeing, hearing, smelling, tasting, touching) that emanate from sources known or unknown. Heat is but an obvious example, as well as electrical conditions of the atmosphere.

Beyond this coordinated sensitivity of the entire nervous system no further or special sense is required. It is superfluous and absurd to postulate mysterious powers of vision, clairaudience, "psychic abilities," and so on, when the normal powers and modus operandi of imagination and memory not only suffice in explanation, but may be investigated experimentally to establish the fact that one's so-called psychic faculties are entirely limited constituently to the contents of the individual memory, just as the constituents of words are limited to the alphabet employed, and my verbal representation is limited to my vocabulary (i.e., my verbal memory), unless I pause to look up or coin a word for an idea that has not yet been incorporated in my verbal organization.

And yet I have had words come to mind and pass over my tongue in experimental conditions, words entirely unfamiliar to me, words in foreign languages, or technical terms that could be found in a dictionary, and some that could not, containing information that I did not myself know, and that was verified as correct. I used familiar syllable, however. I used the familiar alphabet. And even where I inscribed hieroglyphics entirely unfamiliar to me, it was a composition of familiar smaller elements of lines and curves, shapes and angles. The fact still described in terms so vastly misleading and misunderstood as remains that my vision of these things cannot correctly be "psychic," telepathic, and so on. It was nothing whatever but imagination compositing familiar elements of previous sensory experience recorded in memory.

I see and correctly describe a scene ten thousand miles away. (I have done this under experimental conditions as recorded in my files.) I see and describe a future event, which occurs exactly as I described it, with only minor variations. What is lacking or faulty in my description is lacking in my memory. For what so I see? Nothing but my own imagination.

Actually I do not see ten thousand miles away with any form of "vision" whatever. I do not "see" the future. My reception or perception of these things is entirely formless, entirely a "feeling," entirely devoid of image, word, thought or concept. What makes it intelligible to myself or someone else is the activity of my imagination, which endeavors to symbolize, portray or interpret the *feeling.*

And what is the *feeling*? That is the one great mystery. That is the quest. That is the source of all inspiration, the fountainhead of all spiritual gifts, the heart and life of all religion. This is the foundation that science has provided for spiritual understanding — a physiological foundation for a nervous organization that responds to an unknown source or sources of energy in the form of "feelings." These feelings are neurological and physiological, not the activity of a special or occult "sense," but the coordinated activity of the entire nervous organization. The reaction is one of selective stimulation of previously experienced and conditioned reflex arcs of memory. The imagination interprets the "feeling" in terms of memories associated with similar feelings. Thus a complex feeling is broken down into its elements by symbolic representation in an imaginative composite of memory elements. Thereby we "understand" it.

With this explanation we may hope to contribute to a better understanding of mental phenomena stripped of the deceiving terminology of generations of "psychic racketeering." Man's "all-seeing eye" is his imagination, and his imagination sees not beyond his own nerve ends. It sees only the "past" that has been recorded in memory. Still, by this means he may portray what has not yet been recorded (i.e., the future). He may "see" around the world. He may explore the past before his birth in the history of the human race. And why? Because his quivering nerves are open to the universe and susceptible to innumerable feelings. The feelings stimulate and thus clothe themselves in reawakened memory sensations.

Thus we do not see the past, present or future beyond the range of our senses, but we "imagine" it. And if our "feeling" is genuine, our imagination is "true."

Can there be a "false feeling"? Yes, when it is merely the echo of a past feeling aroused by suggestion, association of thought, and memory of words: i.e., intellectual activity in general. The "feeling from outside" can bring you information of a phenomenal nature only when you are able to suspend all internal activity of thought. The "feeling" must have an empty slate to write on. It must be allowed to select your memories, to shape them in your imagination, to choose its own words. The result will be instantaneous, and until you understand the language of feeling, you may not be able to distinguish such formations from your own thoughts. Or, on the other hand, the experience may be so pronounced that you will think you see a "vision," a "spirit," or a "ghost."

You may feel indignant if others call it a hallucination or "imagination," but that is exactly what it is, nothing more. Still, it may be a genuine experience, and the "vision" may be true in every detail within the capacity of your memory to provide the necessary elements.

To help you understand how this can be, and to help you to distinguish between false and true, the wrong and right use of the imagination, the false echo from the genuine feeling, I have taken these pains both to record and to comment on my own personal adventures and research along these lines.

Not everything is easy to explain, but we must avoid attaching the "mystery" to the wrong place. Within all seeds is the "design" of what they will become by growth and development. The creative power exists in the unrecorded. What has been recorded is already "dead." Thus the creative and progressive power in man necessarily manifests as a prophetic power, active in determining what he shall be, and not what he has been.

What has been inherited or already determined as a conditioned reflex is of the past. But what selects or chooses, as in the power of selective absorption of a seed, or the power of selective stimulation in physiological man, is of the "future" in function of "time," which exists solely as a biological phenomenon of succession in growth.

Thus there are innumerable sources of prophetic "feeling" in man that need not be the occasion of any "mystery." In our very careless and inadequate verbal organization we speak of *wishes, wants, desires, appetites, hunger, ambition, aspiration, ideals, hope, anticipation, expectations, faith,* and so on. These terms are neither clearly understood, defined nor differentiated. Means have not been provided to distinguish between those sources of prophetic feeling that are inherent to the structure of our physiological organization — as in the case of animals whose cycle of progressive activity repeats itself each generation — and those sources of prophetic feeling that are not inherent to the individual physiological structure, but which manifest in human progress, which repeats itself in cycles extending through several generations.

To the latter we must attach the "mystery." Self-preservation is not a remarkable phenomenon, but race-preservation is. The man who will fight to preserve himself or his family is not a particularly interesting object of study, but the man who will live his life and give his life for the sake of mankind and human progress is manifesting the

28

mystery that is the religion of mankind. *What is the source of his "feelings"?*

But to return to my own experiences, I have found that whereas "memory is not inherited (i.e., it is not possible to "remember" before we were born in terms of our ability to recall our own sensory experience since birth), we do nevertheless inherit enough of our parents, and through them of past ancestors, to manifest a "feeling" that is capable of arousing parallel memories in our own experience. And thus our imagination may approximate some condition or memory of a parent or ancestor before our birth.

I make this statement on the basis of considerable evidence. Often, however, there is a composite of elements derived from both father and mother, so that the feeling is complex and the resulting imagination a mixture.

Just what caused my mother to dream prophetic dreams while bearing me, and not any of the other children, is something that I do not even attempt to explain. What caused me to dream at the age of seven, going on eight, on a night when I was "reborn" by a distinct psychological change, a dream similar to one my mother dreamed the night I was born one month too soon—that again is something I cannot explain at this stage of the record. And why we both should have dreamed that Herman was hanging on the wall, nailed there as if he had been crucified, might possibly be considered a coincidence, in view of the fact that the symbolism is not unusual in a Catholic family, and if we consider crucifixion to be a symbol of suffering, it could certainly apply to poor Herman, a cripple from birth.

Nevertheless, I can swear that under the circumstances neither Mother nor I breathed a word to Herman about that dream, nor did we tell anyone else, on account of Father's attitude toward such things.

We could not regard the dream as prophetic in a literal sense, since it would be absurd to think that Herman would ever really be found hanging on the wall. At most we could regard it as symbolic, and at worst as symbolic of death. But the dream of a series that had not come true, and it upset her so much at the time that I was precipitated into the world in a premature birth.

Therefore our feelings can be imagined when Herman called Mother one day, after a spell of suffering, and said, *"Mother, hang me on the wall here!"*

Shocked, and thinking he was perhaps delirious, she asked, "And why should I do that?"

He answered, "Because I want to die like Christ died."

Mother said, "But you are not going to die, Herman! Don't talk that way."

He answered, "Yes, I am, Mother."

She put her arm about him, and they prayed together. Then Herman cried himself to sleep.

He never woke up again.

Chapter II

S Herman died just when I felt that I needed him most. Now I was the only boy. I had no brother, and I was indeed alone in the world. For my father was working all day at the large paper mill, my mother was kept busy, the girls had their own interests. I was sent to a Catholic school, but outside of school I had to shift for myself.

And now I made some discoveries. First, that Herman was not "dead."

How did I know? I could not see him, nor could I hear his voice. But I very definitely "felt" his presence. And then, of course, I could imagine him by remembering him, and in my imagination, I could carry on a conversation with him.

Was this really Herman or only my imagination? Well, in the first place, what is the difference between the first sense impression, and the recalling of that sense impression as a memory?

When the reflection of light from Herman that affected my optic nerves affected instead the silver emulsion of a photographic film, we look at the result and say, *"That's Herman."*

I recall the image of Herman in my memory and say to myself, *"It's Herman."*

Certainly I know that it is only my memory, and only in my imagination. But then I think, "Well, anyway, Herman is still alive in my mind."

It was that way when Herman was still alive, when I was off somewhere and he was home. I could remember him then too. But now this was different, because there was a *feeling*. And somehow Herman, or the thought of Herman, seemed to be able to put a life into my memory, and make me imagine things I never imagined before, all through that feeling.

The first time I felt it was a few days after Herman was buried. The feeling came first, and then I thought of Herman.

I imagined him saying, "Well, Joey, I'm still here in your memory, anyway."

I thought, "Now you won't have to stay home all the time, Herman. You can play with me."

Then in my imagination, my memory of Herman said, *"Then don't remember me this way, Joey! I'm not crippled anymore."*

It was then that I realized I was remembering Herman just as he had been when I saw him last. So I changed everything except his face and his eyes and my memory of his voice. Limb by limb I took my memory of Herman and made it over in my imagination, until it could run around as I did.

And then I was so thrilled by the difference that tears came to my eyes. The feeling became so strong that it burst out of my mouth, and I said, "*Thanks!*"

Then something struck me funny, and I said, "Herman, was that me thanking you, or you thanking me?"

Suddenly a joyous feeling filled me, and I laughed with it. I ran out to play, and imagined Herman running out with me. I began to show him all the things he hadn't been able to see or do when he was crippled.

It did not occur to me to regard it as anything other than pure imagination on my part. I did not think Herman's "spirit" was running around with me. I had always carried on conversations in my mind, and now for a while, instead of talking with myself, I talked with a reconstructed memory of Herman in my imagination. The fact that my imaginary and reconstructed brother occasionally said things in my imagination that I did not knowingly put into his mouth was a fact that passed unnoticed by me at the time. I took it for granted as something quite to be expected.

For example, I would go to the woods, and I would imagine Herman saying, "*Well, Joey, we haven't seen any Indians yet.*" And this would remind me that my chief anticipation on leaving Montabaur for the New World was the prospect of Indians. There was first a long coach ride. It was night, and I was the only one of all the passengers who stayed awake. I imagined Indians stopping the horses and saying that they would kill me if I made a sound or woke the rest up.

I thought, "But you were asleep, Herman."

And my imagination of Herman answered, "*Not when you were scalped, Joey. That woke me up.*"

And then I laughed, because I had forgotten that incident, but now I remembered that right while I was in the thick of my imaginary Indians during the coach ride, someone in the coach dropped something that hit me on the head. So vivid were my imaginings that for a moment I thought I had been scalped, and woke Herman up with my war-whoop.

School made me nervous, sitting so still. One day I began to beat a rhythm with my hands and feet. The teacher told me to stop, and asked me what I was doing it for. I couldn't answer her. She said, "Well, if you can do a thing, you can explain why you were doing it. Now tell me!"

All I could say was, "I don't know."

So she struck me over the knuckles with a ruler, and said, "Well, don't do it again, or this ruler will know a better place to hit you."

I sat there stunned and humiliated, with tears blinding my eyes. It was not just the pain on the knuckles. It was worse than that. I had not been long in the school, and I had looked up with admiration at the teacher. I had wanted her to like me, and now she had struck me.

Needing some comfort, I imagined Herman, and said in my mind, "Was that right, Herman? Was it right for her to hit me that way?"

I imagined Herman saying, "*Why didn't you tell her, Joey? Tell her why you were doing that. Go after school and tell her.*"

"But I don't know why."

"*Yes you do.*"

And then it came to me. On the way to America we could not afford a first-class passage, so we were near the engine of the ship during the entire trip. For seventeen days the rhythmic beat of the engine pounded its way into my system, so that whenever I became nervous or restless my feet or fingers unconsciously tapped out the rhythm of the monotonous chugging of the ship's engine.

Then I imagined Herman saying, "*Do you remember how you tied a tin can to a string and let it down over the side of the ship, Joey?*"

Then I thought, "Yes, I would draw it up full of water sometimes. But one day the water in the can was warm. And then it was cold again. I wonder why that was?"

The answer came, "*Ask her. Ask the teacher when you explain about beating your hands and feet.*"

And so I did. She was interested, and talked about it with someone else. Then she told me that when the water I drew up was warm, we were crossing the Gulf Stream. She said she was sorry she had struck my knuckles with the ruler, and would not have done so if I had explained to her, but I wouldn't answer her, and that's why she struck me.

As time passed, I took more and more to wandering through the woods, studying all living things in my own way, speaking to them and making believe that they answered me.

I thought, "*Everything could speak if we could only interpret it.*"
???

By this even as a child, I did not believe that animals and trees could speak the English or any other language of spoken words, or that they had human qualities. (That would have been anthropomorphic!) But I did believe that everything in nature had a "meaning," like a word in the language of Nature, and that this language that we see through our eyes, hear through our ears, smell through our nose, touch with our fingers, and taste with our tongues, was also the language that was in my head when I closed my eyes and ears, and "imagined" things.

This was a language "without words," and this, I thought, was the one language of all the world, the language of thought itself, in which all knowledge could be expressed. I was forced to this language for my own understanding, moving from a country where one language was spoken, to a country where another language was spoken.

So I looked at a tree and understood it. I heard a sound and knew what made it without looking to see. I smelled odors in the woods, and knew what they came from. And then I found that if I touched something with my fingers, I could tell whether anyone else had touched it before me.

How did I know? It was a "feeling." And then I found that if I let that feeling make me "imagine" things without thinking, I could describe who had touched, it, and other things connected with it in the past. As time passed, someone told me, "*What, that's psychometry*. You were able to psychometrize things."

I answered, "But that's silly. It isn't anything but what I feel with my fingers. And then I try to imagine what the feeling means."

And then they would say, "But you described the whole scene exactly, where this object came from. You must see it in order to do that."

But I didn't see it. I saw nothing but my own imagination, nothing but bits and fragments of my own past memories. But what put them together correctly to express the meaning of a *feeling*?

What puts the letters of the alphabet together to form words? What puts words together to form sentences of understanding?

No one could answer me. Nor could I. All I knew was that if I stroked a thing with my fingers until I felt that it was a part of me, like my foot, I could "feel" it, just like my foot.

There is only one way my foot can talk to me, and that is by a feeling. It may be pleasant or unpleasant, hot or cold, comfortable, tired or painful. My own memory tells me why, and what it means. I can't see my foot—it's in my shoe. I can't see my foot even if it's bare. All I can see is the dead skin outside. That's all I can see of anything. All we ever see is the dead skin of things. We never see what anything really is. We can only "feel" it.

If people were going to insist on calling that "seeing," very well then. I could "see" better with the ends of my fingers and with my eyes closed. Also I could "hear" better that way.

To prove it, and to amuse my friends, I would hold my hand high, fingertips in the direction of a distant railway engine five miles away that none of my friends could hear or see. I would say, "It's whistling, only you can't hear it now." Then, "It's coming closer, closer—*now it's going to whistle*: one, two, three…" And *whooo* came the shriek of the engine just after my third count.

"But how did you know?"

"I saw the engineer reach up to pull the whistle."

"How did you see it? We couldn't even see the train yet."

"With my fingers."

"But you can't see with your fingers!"

"Of course not. But that's what you insist on calling it."

"But you must see it in your mind, then. It's second sight. It's clairvoyance."

"Those are just words. And what they mean to you isn't true. I don't see that train and that engineer at all. I'm just imagining it. What I see in my mind is a train I remember looking at one time from close up. The engineer in my mind is one who waved at me one time. That may be him, but I don't think so, and I don't know. It's the engineer in my memory and not the engineer in the train that starts reaching for the handle to pull the whistle. When he starts reaching, I start counting. That's all there is to it."

"But what makes the engineer in your imagination start reaching at the right time?"

"I don't know."

"Well, I don't understand it at all. You're a strange one, and no fooling."

I didn't like this. I would say, "You could do it too, but you don't try."

One time I said, "I'll show you. Let me put your coat over your head. Hold up your hand. A cloud is going to pass over the sun. You tell me the minute it does. Then after a few minutes tell me when the sun breaks through again."

When this was done successfully, I asked, "How did you know?"

"Because I could feel the warmth of the sun on my skin. When it was cool, I knew the cloud had covered the sun. When it was warm again, I knew the cloud had passed."

"Well, what's strange about that? It was a feeling in your hand and you knew what it meant."

"But that's different."

"No, it isn't different. Not in the way you mean. Of course it's different, but it's the same thing."

"What a way to talk! It's the same thing only different! That's about as clear as mud, Joey."

So I stopped trying to explain things for a while. I didn't know enough about them myself.

In school, things didn't go so well. Not that it was hard for me, or that I got poor marks. But they didn't teach the things I wanted to know about, and they didn't talk the language I understood best.

What I wanted, I couldn't express or explain at that time. My soul cried out dumbly what others before me and after me found words to say: "*Give me the things, not words about things. Give me the thoughts, not words about thoughts.*"

So I could not bring myself to study then, and in a whole lifetime of research I have never been able to study since — to study things and nature, yes, but not words and books.

Thirty years later I dreamed a dream of being a schoolboy again, kneeling on a dusty corner asleep, while the other pupils worked their heads off studying the essential oils. When recess came, I went out and had a fine time, but the rest were too tired.

This was symbolic of my whole life. I have seen more lives blasted and stunted by brain-cramming than by utter ignorance. Hence, I have always preached against tiring out the colt in practice before the hour set for the race.

Man's worst enemy is his memory, he has misused it. It was never meant to be a trunk into which to pack a lot of words and opinions. It was meant to record experience as a sample-case, an alphabet of nature's language, like stringing a harp or piano, one string of each tone. Then any melody in the world of music can be played on it. And even from a distance the vibration of another tone will produce a vibration in my instrument, if I possess a string of like pitch to respond to it. I do not need to see, hear, smell, taste or touch it. The string in my piano is going to vibrate if someone strikes the same string on another piano at a distance.

But the string of my piano is not going to vibrate if I use the piano as a trunk and pack it full of words. The words are going to bang around on the strings so I cannot hear anything else.

As long as I didn't learn from books, as long as I kept my memory from recording anything but direct experience, experiment and observation, and as long as I could seal off a part of my brain for a vocabulary but refrain from using it in my thinking, then my thinking was not confined to my head. I could think with my whole body, with every nerve and organ, and then I would know the truth — for they would not lie to me as men did, and as books did, using words.

I wanted the truth to select its own words, and not for men to try to shape ideas of truth in my brain with their words. This would not be true, and it was impossible ever for it to be true, for that is not what truth is.

Every argument I ever heard was caused by someone trying to shape the truth by words, instead of allowing the words to be shaped by truth.

Fervently and deeply I wanted the truth, and I could see that none of the teachers knew the truth, and none of the books told the truth. It was nothing but words, and words about words. Brick by brick, word by word, I saw the wall being built around us children to seal us for life into one room of our brain, with only two windows, our eyes, safely guarded with prison bars of words stronger than steel, that also kept out most of the light, with every other gate of the mind carefully sealed by a word, so that no feeling could be arrived at, save through a word first, like putting gloves on our hands, shoes on our feet, spectacles on our eyes, muffs on our ears, and a woolen padding on every nerve end so we would be cut off from the quivering, life-giving pulsations of direct contact with the truth.

So I revolted. I tore down the wall of words, threw off my shoes, both physically and mentally, and walked barefoot even where the stones were sharp and painful.

I went on alone in rain and thunderstorms, praying to God to let me feel the truth that no one could tell me in words. I promised that if He could make me "feel" the right things to do, I would always obey those feelings, instead of what other people told me to do when one person said one thing, and another said another.

When I got out alone like this, a strange feeling would sometimes come over me. When it did, then as far as I could see, everything, instead of being outside my head, seemed to be inside my head.

Looking out over a marsh where the frogs were croaking, I would hear them as if they were inside my head. They seemed to be a part of me, and I would amuse myself by pointing in a certain direction, saying, *"One, two, three — now!"* And a big bullfrog would croak from where I pointed.

So far as the evidence of personal experience is concerned, it does not answer the question whether the seeming ability to "cause" a frog to croak at will was a real one, or whether I predicted the croak.

This is merely illustrative. The problem comes up repeatedly in my records, as this type of phenomena is now an established fact with a sufficient number of reliable witnesses, so that the solution to this problem is one of the most fundamental considerations in the fields of science, philosophy, and religion. To what extent does the mind "make" things happen, and to what extent does the mind foresee what is going to happen? Does the mind create thought, or is it acted upon by thought?

Has man deceived himself by extending his conception of biological time beyond the sphere of its function in nature? Does cause precede or follow effect? Have we perhaps gotten the cart before the horse in thinking that the cause comes first because of our manner of recording biological time in a reflective function of memory, where things are naturally reversed, as in a mirror or any other phenomenon of reflection? How is it, for example, that in dreams the sound that caused a dream wakes you up, and that the dream precedes the sound that has "caused" it?

Then again, here is an acorn. Overhead I see the oak tree from which it fell. I know that if I plant it, it will grow into another oak tree, and if I gather all the acorns from that, I can prove that within my hand at this moment I hold the means to produce a whole forest of oak trees.

The past is "outside," over my head. The acorn has left it forever. Yet in the same moment I imagine the future forest of oak trees, and I know that at this very minute, though the chemical constituents of that oak tree of the future are in the air I breathe, and in the soil beneath my feet, I know that the true cause of that future forest lies in the palm of my hand, inside the seed (in the future of that growth), and not in the tree overhead, (its past), from which it has departed forever.

The cause of a thing is in action or a function, and not a position or sequence in space or in biological time. The old oak tree produced the acorn in my hand, but now the active cause of the future oak tree is in that acorn as its own future, which becomes manifest by selective absorption in growth. The old oak tree is cut off from any possible function as a cause of growth in the new tree. The power of creation is the future biologically. The past is the memory of the body, the future is the memory of the seed. My dream precedes the sound that causes it, just as my backward is forward in the mirror, for a dream is a reflex of memory.

And likewise when by shock of emergency or will of intent and earnest desire we suspend our logic and reason, and revolt from our walls of words, then only our raw nerves are exposed to nature. We think with our spine, our hands, our feet, our skin. What is outside of us is now part of us, inside. We are a waking dream. We are conscious on the other side of the fence. Our actions precede what causes them.

I say, *One, two, three* — and the train whistles. I say, *One, two, three* — and a frog croaks. And one time, before eleven witnesses who are all still living as I write this (this was later in life), in the midst of a storm I said, "Look at that tree, if you want to see something. Suppose I told you I could make lightning strike that tree. Would you believe me? Of course not. But watch it. *One, two, three* —

And no one was more astonished than I when a bolt of lightning split the tree before our eyes, for I was in a "waking dream" at the time, having abandoned myself to the spirit and enjoyment of the storm. The lightning bolt broke my state of contemplation, or whatever you may choose to call it, hence I was astonished at the fulfillment of what I had been only half conscious of saying.

This may sound incredible, but I assure you that it is a fact of experience before witnesses, and only one of several thousand cases embodying the same principle. None of my witnesses is of a type to grant me power to cause a particular tree to be split by lightning at the third count of my finger. There are, therefore, only a few other possible conclusions:

1. That as in a dream, my speech preceded the sound or event that caused it, in which case, our conception of, and relation to, "time" needs deeper investigation and perhaps drastic revision.
2. That neither my speech nor the event was the cause of the other, both being the effect of a common cause, viz., the power

that caused the event also called my attention to it, and through me the attention of others before it happened. Either 1 or 2 with variations could be embodied in a theory of prophecy or prevision. We could state another possibility:

3. That the cause of my speech was not the power that caused the event, but rather a power in myself, or acting upon myself, which could foresee the event without any causal connection whatever.

Still further, 2 might be clarified by limiting the "power" to a purely material nature. For example, we say that "instinct" causes muskrats to "hole in" just before a storm, but reflex conditioned by a change or degree of atmospheric pressure associated with a consequence would account for it.

Moreover, I have turned one of my laboratories into a large electrical condenser, with an electronic ohmmeter connected between a metallic roof and the ground. The radiation resistance of this portion of space started building up one rainy day, and as the needle mounted higher and higher, till it could record no more, at one hundred million ohms, I knew without any "mental phenomena" that lightning was going to strike in the vicinity. It struck within two minutes after the capacity of the meter had been reached. Who is to say that the human nervous organization is not as sensitive as one built by man's hands?

Still, that would not account for picking the right tree. Nor did the meter tell me what my nerves now did after the crash, when I asked, *"Did anyone get the horses in before it started to rain?"*

My assistant said, "I don't know. Why? Shall I go and find out?"

I said, "The bolt was so close it made me feel as if I were a horse. I imagined a horse leaping into the air and falling down dead."

My assistant went back to the barn and found that the horses were not in, as the rain had come on so suddenly. One of the other men was standing in the barn looking out at the downpour that followed the crash.

He said, "Yes, I know the horses should have been brought in, but I was just starting back to the pasture for them when it started. I'm just waiting for it to let up a little."

So both went back to look for the horses, and found two of them dead. One of them had leaped a six-foot fence and was several feet away without any tracks leading there.

In this case and others like it, I have had delicate instruments in my laboratory, in a temperature-controlled room, which correlated in their functions with outdoor temperature and weather changes, but slightly in advance of the outdoor effects. It became evident that the instruments were being acted upon at once by forces that a little later, sometimes five to twenty minutes, brought about the outdoor changes, thus enabling us to predict them by a small margin. Changes in atmospheric and electrical conditions, for example, preceded local meteorological effects, as also atmospheric tidal effects on temperature changes.

Thus it seems reasonable to believe that the human nervous system might be able to detect conditions on the same basis. But this will not account for all the phenomena observed. The imminence of a lightning bolt might be felt, but what explains pointing to the tree it will strike, and timing the flash to the second? What explains the fact that when a real horse leaped into the air and dropped dead, a memory of a horse in my imagination did likewise?

And if what causes a frog to croak can act more quickly upon my nervous system when "attuned" to it, giving me time to count three before the frog reacts, how does this work with the engineer tooting his whistle, or a man doing what I say he is going to do without his knowledge of the fact, so that the power of direct suggestion is eliminated? Did I make him do it? Did I foresee that he was going to do it? Or were we both acted upon by some unknown third factor that caused me to predict the act, and the other man to fulfill it?

All that is established experimentally (and this I have done thousands of times in the course of my research) is a relation of sequence with respect to the biological time of me and my witnesses. (1) I state what is going to happen. (2) It happens. Is 1 the cause of 2? Is 2 the cause of 1? Are both 1 and 2 the effect of a common cause? Is the relation entirely fortuitous, i.e., just a matter of "chance" or "coincidence"? Or is there some other explanation?

For example, is it possible that our conception of causality is in error, and that prevision does not imply predestination, that prophecy and "free will" are perfectly compatible if not identical, in the sense that free will requires dimension in biological time?

If free will on the part of Deity or man requires the setting in motion of processes that require or constitute time, the determination and the fulfillment of free will would be separated by a time interval that may vary from an instant in which you ask your neighbor at the table to pass the butter, up to a lifetime that may be cut short if it is

41

your "free will" to end it, or to violate the laws of health in slow suicide of neglect.

In any case the aim of the bullet can be altered up to the moment the trigger is pulled, but once pulled, the bullet is on its way to a target that was not predestined until the release of nature's forces beyond man's control.

Since in every case free will does involve a time interval, however short or long, between its determination and its fulfillment, it is perfectly possible that prophecy is based on immediate knowledge or foreknowledge of the execution of free will in a determination that thus permits the manifestation of prophecy in perfect harmony with free will. Yet this has been considered in philosophic and theological difficulty of insurmountable nature, whereas it is in nature and human experience no difficulty at all.

???

The only difference between scientific and intuitive prediction is that in science the execution of an act of free will is known by observation or intention, and that in the case of intuition it is "sensed" or "felt" in a way no more "occult" or mysterious than the function of an insect's antennae, but in man by the coordinated activity and sensitivity of his entire nervous organization. And whereas science is based on reflective analysis and comparison of sensory perceptions and memories of past sensory perceptions, intuition is based on the automatic and synthetic coordination of man's entire physiological organization, wherein by selective stimulation of reflex arcs (called "memory") a series of "feelings" is transformed into an activity of imagination that constitutes understanding and provides a basis for responsive activity of the motor or sympathetic nervous system.

If thoughts may be changed, environments may be changed. If environments may be changed, destiny may be changed, for there is a constant adaptation to environments. So "destiny" may be altered by one who knows the laws by which he can do so intelligently. This knowledge constitutes "free will" and involves "moral responsibility." Not everyone acquires or exercises it, hence the present condition of the world today.

Most of us do what we do today because of the momentum of yesterday, or by reaction to stimuli, without exercising the ability to resist or suppress that reaction. Thus we are governed by past and present (i.e., memory and sensory reaction), which perpetuates vicious circles, retards progress, and prolongs undesirable conditions.

Whereas the exercise of "free will" consists of, and entirely depends upon, a consideration of and preparation for "tomorrow."

The present moment is too late to exercise this prerogative with any expectation of altering the present moment. We can alter our future in cooperation with nature's laws, by considering between two possible courses of action, and choosing not merely the course of action leading to the "most desirable" result, but the criterion by which we shall evaluate that "desirability."

The mistake many make is in considering the "will" and "desire" as simple things. They are not simple but complex. It is possible to change the will by "willing to will," and to change a desire by "desiring to desire" (i.e., by changing one's criterion).

Man has two sources of desire and will that are founded in two distinct physiological systems of conditioned reflexes. One of these he shares in common with all animals. The other is distinctly the endowment and distinguishing characteristics of man. Neither of these two systems is "free," insofar as the reflexes have already been formed and conditioned. The freedom that is denied to animals and enjoyed by man is the power and the necessity by reflection to create and modify the growth and development of further reflex arcs (i.e., to make or modify tendencies, habits or hopes).

If we call this reflective and representative ability "intellect," then this is the seat and source, and *modus operandi* of individuality and free will. For the intellect may lend its aid as a modifier to either one of man's two sources of will, or, man's two sources of will may engage in conflict for the possession of the intellect. The one is the will of experience, habit, instinct. The other is the selective development of latent possibilities in the seed. One is the voice of the past, the other of the future. Free will is the gift of prophecy, and the gift of prophecy is free will.

The moment you lose hope and faith, your destiny is established regardless of your will, like a bullet shot from a rifle that cannot be turned from its course. As long as your optimistic hand holds opportunity, you govern "fate." But if you drop it through doubt, carelessness or pessimism, you are in the hand of fate's "destiny," not your own will.

Thus religion, as the guarantor of hope and the guardian of faith, is our only organized insurance of freedom and free will. A wholly dogmatic and authoritarian religion, however, is a religion in name only, a speculative system of beliefs, not an operative and phenomenal function of faith.

43

Free will is the power. What man believes to be his "will" is but a dam for the capture and use of this power. All is right until he uses his willpower the wrong way.

This is the power of the individual, of governing the polarity of his desires by commanding the animal propensities or the spiritual sentiments. Thus he determines which shall predominate, according to whether he allows himself to respond to instinct (past), or to be influenced by intuition or inspiration (future).

Man's only escape from this fundamental conflict of choice has been a disastrous one for him (i.e., to reject both instinct and intuition), thus confining himself to the independent operations of the intellect (i.e., to a world of reflective and verbal representations).

Within this sphere of purely intellectual activity, the truth is entirely irrelevant, with respect to the physiological and psychological consequences of the reflective and representative activities of the brain and nervous system. The multifarious combinations of memory sensations create states of mind, and motivates action, without regard to their "truth" or "falsity" with respect to any criteria whatever.

Until we embody the physiological laws of thought in a logic capable of correlating language with life, more philosophic speculation is barren and without any probability of correspondence with truth.

Our only practical physiological means of insuring the correspondence of our imaginative activity with external conditions is by the use of special sensory organs in the acquisition of experience, the exercise of immediate observation, and the invention of apparatus in experiments. This is science.

???

Our only practical means of insuring the correspondence of our imaginative activity with external or internal conditions beyond the capacity and ability of our sensory organs to acquire experience, to exercise immediate observation, or to invent and apply activity of the entire nervous system as "antennae" in the acquisition of knowledge by "feelings," which are to be understood only by the selective stimulation of memory elements in the activity of imagination from which all independent operations of the intellect have been rigidly excluded.

This is the domain of religion, not as a system of speculative belief, but as an operative function of intuition and faith that involves and includes the inspiration of all the so-called spiritual gifts,

44

including prophecy, and all types of mental phenomena to which have been falsely attributed occult or psychic connotations.

The exercise of the latter to the exclusion of the former produces but half-men and half-truths: i.e., mystics and mysticism. The exercise only of the former produces but half-men and half-truths: i.e., skeptics and skepticism.

The materialism of science and the spiritualism of religion are each in themselves incapable of embracing the whole man or the whole truth. It is only the two together, functioning in one man, not in separate men, that produces the capacity of mankind to a universal consciousness, coordination and understanding.

Chapter III

It was shortly after the time in my boyhood when I revolted against the schoolroom, and turned to nature instead for my lessons. I would play truant and go off alone in a storm, talking back at the thunder as if it were God speaking.

I would say, "If I call upon you, and still fail to find the truth and the true religion, it will not be my fault, because we have been told, '*Ask and ye shall receive; seek and ye shall find; knock and it shall be opened unto you.*'"

I would say to myself, "If there is such a thing as a *Holy Spirit*, let me feel it. I don't want anyone to tell me about it anymore. All I ask is *let me feel it myself*, and then I will know."

I said this, not doubting, not asking for "proof," but as a hungry child demanding food, not words about food and pictures of good things to eat.

When I thought this way, a tingle would start in my spine that chilled me from head to foot, and then a feeling would go out to the end of every nerve in my body, as if my heart were pumping warm wine instead of blood. I would feel a glow all over.

I would say, "Thank you, God!" And then the tears would come to my eyes because I was happy. I never told anyone about this. People wondered why I was always happy, and always whistling and singing. This was why.

That was in the spring, and when summer came, I was sent to a farm to work for a man who was kind to me. I tended the cows every day, taking them a long way out on a road where I staked them to graze. This was the school for me. I learned more doing this than I had learned all year in school.

When it was time to go back to school again, I became so nervous and restless that I was allowed to leave school and work in a spring shop for a dollar and twenty-five cents per week, to help my parents.

Thus I left school at the age of thirteen, and have never been inside of one since, except later in life as moderator and director of local school boards.

As for religion, I was absent from churches as well as schoolrooms, and for the same reason. I had found outside in nature, and within myself, what they did not, nor could not give me.

I have in the course of my life investigated every religion known to man on earth, past or present. I have enjoyed close friendships with leaders and laymen in all faiths — with priests, rabbis, and ministers of many denominations. And I must say that when I dug beneath the words and the various intellectual representations of doctrines and concepts, I found the same fundamental, universal faith by which man sustains a relation to his Creator and the spirit of truth in a function of neutral activity or consciousness other than "intellect."

And when as a scientist I convinced myself of the irrelevance of truth with respect to the physiological and psychological consequences of the operations of the intellect, a conclusion immediately follows that dispenses with all argument. It does not make any difference whether or not the doctrines, the concepts, and the verbal representations are *true*, so long as the physiological and psychological consequences are favorable to man's spiritual progress: i.e., if they lead the various types of intellect (to which the various doctrines are helpful) to the establishment of a relation with truth in a function of faith that is more fundamental than belief: i.e., an operative, not a speculative relation with the creative reality of God, or truth.

I have therefore devoted my life to the experimental investigation and study of the scientific foundations of the spiritual verities that are of necessity and by virtue of the essential unity of mankind in common with all religions as the essence of a universal Christianity.

Because I have found these spiritual verities to be operative and not speculative, and because in my own experience I have found that they operate in mankind through a physiological function of faith, and not an intellectual function of speculative belief, I urge the support of all religions with emphasis on the faith they have in common, rather than the doctrinal beliefs by which they differ, and which a study of the history of religion and the history of mankind will reveal to have been the necessary expressions of intellectual variations to insure the perpetuation of the more essential elements of man's physiological relation with truth through the non-intellectual operations of a living, universal faith.

At the age of fourteen I went to Chicago with my father. My mother and sister followed later. This was during the World's Fair, and my father was employed in connection with one of the exhibits. Later, my parents had a bakery and a milk depot in the city. I got up early every morning when it was still dark to deliver milk. By this time my father was a citizen of the United States, and was employed at the government appraisal store. Not going to school, I always had some time for myself outside of work. I used it experimenting, and my mechanical, electrical, and chemical "inventions" were a source of great bother and worry to my mother, who was afraid of fires and explosions.

From time to time I secured work in various trades, in search of different kinds of experience. When I was fifteen, I worked for a company that made window screens. Here I invented and constructed a machine for stapling the screening onto the frames.

I used to dream of having a wonderful shop, fitted out with every tool imaginable, so I could make things. I wanted also a chemical and electrical research laboratory and workshop. All of these daydreams materialized, though some of them many years later.

During this time I began to have experiences with regard to which space here permits the inclusion of only a few examples. One time while working for the Hall Safe & Lock Company, I was sent out to dismantle the lock of a safe that had been blown open by safecrackers. I placed a drift in position and raised my hammer to strike it.

Now came the first experience in my life in which something happened in my arm that I could not account for as an act of will or reflex to my own thoughts. With hammer in mid-air, something held my hand so that I could not hit the drift. The feeling was not as if some outside force held my arm, but something inside the muscles. They refused to make the motion I had instructed them to do by the impulse of my brain and the reflex of habit. So I examined the lock to see if perhaps I was hitting it in the wrong place to accomplish what I had to do.

Satisfied that I was hitting it in the right place, I raised my hammer again but could not bring myself to strike the drift. Then down my arm came the "feeling" that there was something there I shouldn't hit. So I pulled the drift out again, and behind it I found a dynamite cartridge that had been placed there by the safecrackers, and that had not yet been exploded.

This was the first of many similar experiences. Again and again throughout my life, I would have lost fingers, hands, arms, legs, and life itself were it not for an independent action of my muscles in making a movement I did not direct, or in refusing to make a movement that I did direct.

What was it, within myself or in the universe, that had the power to move my muscles without my own will, or to prevent them from carrying out what I had every reason to believe to be my will? I did not know. All I could swear to was that it happened not once or twice, but again and again. Now, at the age of seventy it still happens — but always as a last extremity.

In later years, I learned to look for a feeling and to obey it in time to direct my own course of prevention. But failing this, "something else" took over, and as a result of it, in a long life of activity, of travel, of driving various kinds of vehicles, operating all kinds of machinery, I have never had a serious accident, but innumerable narrow escapes, all owing to some kind of purposive or automatic reflex of self-preservation.

Problem: What is it? I have friends, bless them, who seem to think that such questions are answered by muttering a name. I demonstrate to them the fact that I can attract and repel a piece of steel "at a distance" by means of another piece of steel concealed in my hand.

I say, "There you behold an invisible force. You can't see it, smell it, taste it, hear it, or touch it. Yet I can cause that piece of steel to roll away from me or roll toward me at will. What is it?"

Secure behind their wall of words, such people say, "Why, any school boy knows what that is! It's *magnetism.*"

"Do you know what magnetism is?"

"It's what you're using to make that piece of steel move."

"But do you know what it is."

"Well, no. Does anybody?"

"That's what I'm trying to find out. Very few admit they don't know until I drive them to it. They solve all the problems of the universe by means of magic names."

As long as things have names people are satisfied. As long as they can mutter a sound or draw signs on a blackboard, or stir the sign and the sound up out of their memory, that is all that is necessary. Look around the world and hear the torrent of mutterings like a perpetual hailstorm. See the rivers of ink flowing onto tons and tons of paper. Man has built ships for himself out of paper, and sails out into the universe on a river of ink blown by the breath of empty words. Then when the ship of his illusions collapses, he finds himself in total ignorance. For now, without words he knows nothing. But had he not deceived himself, he might now, without words, have known all.

Some of my friends do not like this line of thought. "You can't do without words," they argue, "You yourself speak and write every day of your life. You have written a newspaper column for years, using perhaps four or five million words. You can't convey your thoughts without naming words."

To this I answer, "But I don't think in words, and I don't think with the part of my brain that remembers words. I'm trying to break down the wall of words that holds you prisoner, and unbar the gates of your mind that words have sealed shut. I'm trying to show you that your fingers, your muscles, your spine, and every organ and cell in your body knows more that you do, and that here is nothing more ignorant in the human anatomy than an educated brain that has barred every gate of the mind except that associated with verbal reflex.

"A man with such a brain is nothing more than a piece of machinery. His voice but a phonograph record. It is beyond his comprehension, because he has no comprehension—only fixed ideas, concepts anchored to words. He cannot believe because he cannot personally experience what it means to stretch out a quivering antenna of nerves that pick up feelings and transform them from electric currents, which stir up visual and verbal memories and reactions, into the echoes of a past, a living, or a future voice or scene."

It is not the knowledge of the brain that holds the hand from hitting a dynamite cartridge that can't be seen, or that causes one to hesitate and miss the plane or train that is going to crash. What is it? Are we going to "fix" it with a name?"

A name is nothing without a meaning. A meaning is impossible without understanding, and an understanding is impossible merely on the basis of a chain-reaction in our verbal memory. An understanding is possible only on the basis of neural activity in direct response to the object or subject of that understanding—not merely a twitch in a brain cell that awakens the memory of a few words, but the coordination of the entire physiological and neurological organization.

How glibly the vocabularies of philosophies and ideologies, of sciences and theologies flow from the tongue! And how many know anything? How many really understand anything? Very few can define the words they use, and when they do, the words are dead.

We speak of *hunches, intuition, presentiments, precognition, extrasensory perception, inspiration, psychometry, spiritualism, clairvoyance, telepathy, divination, superstition, faith, the Holy Spirit, God.* All these words are used to talk "about" something. None of the words, as defined and understood by anyone I have ever talked with, adequately represent what they are talking about, because the words

50

have not been coined by men who know or understand adequately what they are trying to name.

Public conception of the terms has been deformed by the operation of "psychic racketeers" who have capitalized on the crudity and the hunger of people for truth, by deceiving them with tricks. I have investigated these things and I know all these tricks. One of the purposes of this commentary is to attempt to rescue the truth, and to restore understanding and faith in man's God-given spiritual gifts, so that "each may prophesy, that each may be comforted" for himself without being deceived by charlatans and false prophets, and without being dependent upon the self-assumed authority of others for what he may seek and find and feel and know himself.

One day when I was walking down the street, I felt very blue and discouraged without knowing why. This was unusual for me, because I was ordinarily contented and cheerful, if not happy, in those days. This was a new feeling and I could see no reason for it. I did not know of anything that would make me blue. I felt that way all day, and I could not identify or interpret the feeling. My imagination was no help to me now.

That night my father asked me what ailed me. I said I did not know. He insisted that if I was unhappy, there must be a reason for it, and he wanted to know what it was.

The moment he asked the question the answer was there. It was something about my father that made me feel unhappy. Now my imagination had something to work on, but I didn't want to tell him about it, because now in his presence I felt and imagined that he was going to die, and that was what made me feel so upset and unhappy.

However, he forced me to tell him that I was afraid he was going to die suddenly, within two weeks. And then he punished me for dabbling with such nonsense, and said he thought I had gotten over that sort of thing long ago.

For the moment my father convinced me that I was wrong, because I hoped I was wrong. So for the next few days I tried to put it out of my mind. At least I never spoke of it. But early in the second week my father came down suddenly with a fever that developed into typhoid pneumonia. At the end of two weeks he was gone.

Overnight my boyhood was over. I was now the only man of the family. I went to work to help support my mother and sister. Shortly after my father's death my mother met friends who attended "spiritualist" meetings. She accompanied them one time, and told us at home of what she had heard and seen. I could not believe her, and was curious to find out how much of it was true.

So I went to see this medium of whom my mother and her friends were speaking so enthusiastically. I was sorely disappointed. Before the séance was over, I had detected and knew how all of the tricks were done by which the public was being deceived.

Here I do not wish to be misunderstood. The fact that I found one medium fraudulent was not grounds enough to form a judgment that all mediums were fraudulent. But the fact that the first medium I ever met was fraudulent is sufficient to explain why I avoided all séances on general principles until I made up my mind to investigate and expose the tricks for the sake of the truth that did exist, and that I felt needed no "*stage trimmings*."

Later on I met a number of very sincere mediums whom I judged to be honest, but to some extent self-deceived. Also I met a few who confessed their tricks, and justified them by saying, "We use a trick to make people believe a truth, because the people cannot understand, and will not believe the truth without the trick."

I cannot here include details of my later investigations along these lines, but I must say that while my own personal experience convinced me absolutely of the truth of immortality, the reality of survival, the fact that death does not end all, in the reality of a type of communication based on "feeling" such as might take place also between two living persons who are attuned by bonds of love and affection, I have yet to be convinced of any form of "materialism," trumpet blowing, slate-writing, spirit-photography, and so on. And at the time I am speaking of it, in the city of Chicago, this is just about all that spiritism consisted of. And in every instance where I was a witness, I privately exposed the trick and revealed how it was done. And I can assure you it was not done by a "spirit."

Yet at the same time I frequently "felt" the presence of my father. The feeling revived a memory, and I could imagine him walking along beside me. I could "talk" with him by saying something and "imagining" what he might say in return.

If I had been willing to deceive myself as some mediums were, I could have said, "I see my father, and he tells me so and so." But I did not see my father. What I "saw" was a memory of my father. He did not speak to me at all. The words were out of my own verbal memory, and I put them into the mouth of the memory of my father in my imagination. Then how could I explain it when the memory of my father in my imagination told me things I did not myself know, and that only my mother knew?

It all comes back to the "feeling" again. So far as I could see, the only link between the living and the dead, the seen and the unseen, was a "feeling," just as the only link between two telegraph operators is the current in the wires. The click that the receiver hears is not the click that the sender hears. It is a different" click." You do not hear the voice of your friend over the telephone; what you hear is a vibration in your receiver that sounds like your friend's voice.

Perhaps there do exist people who think that the voices they hear in their radio are the voices of the broadcasters a thousand miles away, but of course that is not true. What we hear is the vibration of a diaphragm in the Magnavox, and not the vibration of the larynx of the person who is speaking.

And perhaps people who watch the images on a television screen are really under the illusion that they are seeing the faces, forms, and movements of the players in the broadcasting studio. If so, they are deceiving themselves, like the mediums who think they "see" spirits and "hear" voices.

You see nothing on a television screen but the variations of intensity of a spot of light, which is moving with such great rapidity that it creates the illusion of sustained vision. The distribution of light intensity throughout the field, being determined by the reflection of light from the players and scene in the studio, deceives your optic nerves into believing you "see" the players. But how is this done from a distance, "without any wires" and "through the air"?

Answer that and you will have an adequate explanation of all so-called mental phenomena—with the sympathetic nervous system as antennae, the imagination as amplifier and television screen. What you see in your mind's eye of imagination is nothing but the flickering composite of one's own memory element.

Whether or not this "means" anything more than your memory, depends entirely on whether you can turn the switch in your nervous system that reverses the current, so that the nervous system is acting on the memory, and not the memory on the nervous system.

If the nervous system is acting on the memory, then your "feeling" manifests in imagination by selective stimulation of memory elements to form an "image," or a succession of remembered sounds. Then, just as a seed manifests what it contains by selective absorption of chemical elements for the soil and air, so does a thought or "truth," or a "spirit," or whatever you prefer to call it, manifest in a "feeling"

53

that translates itself by selective stimulation of memory elements or motor elements, into imagination or action.

At least this was my early understanding of the matter. At no time have I ever had evidence that a "thought" or "spirit" could move anything other than a human organism and nervous system. At no time have I ever had evidence that either a thought or a spirit could be "seen" or photographed. At no time have I ever "heard" a thought or a spirit. All I can state from personal experience is that whenever a feeling originates in my nervous system without internal cause, whenever I succeed at the same time in eliminating all other influence, suspending all other sensory reactions; i.e., when I *stop thinking* independently and allow my thought to be "shaped" by the feeling, then what takes place in my imagination (though it remain only imagination, composited of my own memories) nevertheless corresponds with some external reality or event, past, present, or future, without any limitation in space or time save the decided and very troublesome and insurmountable limitation of what my memory contains to contribute to the visualized representation that is the foundation of my understanding.

If this view disappoints any follower of fraudulent spiritism, let him then take comfort in the conclusion that though a "spirit message" may not be a direct contact of a loved one, neither is the voice over the radio. But you recognize the voice and understand its intimacy. Why not the thought of a comforting mother in the "beyond"?

Of course it's nothing but your "imagination." But your imagination will tell you the truth if you seek with a prayer (tuning in), and if you will stop thinking with your brain and offer up every nerve from the top of your head to the tips of your fingers and toes, for inspiration. What is inspiration? First, it's a "feeling," and then the feeling paints a picture, sings a song, writes a book, or solves a problem that changes the course of history.

One medium said to me, "I realize all that, but if I tell my people that I only imagine what their deceased loved ones are saying, will they believe me? No, I have to work a trick, and pretend that the spirit writes it on a slate directly. I can't admit that my finger does the writing."

But to this view I could not agree. The search for truth is far more thrilling, more comforting and more profitable here and forever than any imagined thrill or advantage to be gained by deception or self-deception.

Nor could I feel that this was something to "dabble" with, like a plaything. My friends would talk about books on the subject, and tell me that I ought to read this one or that one. But every time I was tempted to do so, a "feeling" would stop me. Just as I was stopped from hitting the drift with my hammer when there was a dynamite cartridge behind it and I didn't know it.

The only book I was able to open without this feeling was the Bible, and there I found the whole subject covered in the 12th chapter of the first epistle of the Corinthians, "Concerning spiritual gifts," and the fourth chapter of John: "*Beloved, believe not every spirit but try them whether they are of God, for many false prophets have gone forth into the world.*"

???

So when my mother and her friends became interested in "table-tipping" and kindred phenomena, I didn't want any part of it. Later, I investigated various forms of "automatic writing," and the phenomena of hypnosis and self-hypnosis to an extent that does not permit inclusion in this record. For reasons given in the connection, I did not feel it advisable to experiment along those lines.

All hypnosis is fundamentally self-hypnosis. No man has the power to hypnotize another against his will, if one exerts that will. All that a "hypnotist" is able to do is to contrive by psychological tricks to secure the willingness and cooperation of the subject. The "power" is in the subject, not in the operator, and the success of the operator depends largely upon securing the confidence, complete trust, or fear of the subject.

Ninety per cent of the people in the world today have spent the largest portion of their lives in various stages of self-hypnosis. The production of these states of mind in the people has been the objective of organized efforts on an incredible scale throughout the world. I have witnessed two World Wars that were directly due to states of self-hypnosis induced in masses of people by the organized efforts and propaganda of small groups of men. We have lived to witness the greatest psychological crime of all history. War would be impossible if we could break the spell of self-hypnosis that holds the people of the world in subjection to false ideas, ideologies, personalities and words, in a state of hypnosis produced by psychological tricks. We must expose these psychological tricks. But that is another story.

So many experiences I had when a young man made me realize that the ready response in my make-up was due to my harp of experience, such as it was, and that whatever confusion and error

55

came into the picture was due to what I lacked in this respect. So I made deliberate efforts to enlarge and perfect this instrument of understanding. Each tool or instrument mastered, added so many more strings, enabling me to give an opinion based upon absolute knowledge. And as I continued to add to this supply of strings, I found a readier response within myself when seeking knowledge by intuition, or endeavoring to interpret knowledge acquired only through the transference of "feelings" from others, or from sources unknown.

I would meet a stranger, for example, and as an experiment attempt to describe his father, who would be totally unknown to me, or some other person he might be thinking of. The correct description, of course, is recorded in his mind, and if I have registered one thousand faces in my own memory, there will be one among these that will now be recalled from my memory by the "feeling" I get from the stranger. This provides me with an imaginative description as nearly as possible like the one in his mind, but which I can sense only in terms of facial characteristics recorded in my own memory in connection with faces I have seen.

These things were thus all clear to me early in life, and I could demonstrate them. But there was one thing that long remained a question mark in my mind, and that was the anatomy of prophetic intuition. For in my own experience, the difference between past and future was that I appeared to get the information of the past as an inductive activity of my mind, while the case of prophetic intuition, it seemed as if I were in the future coming back (deductive), and with it a sort of reverential awe, a kind of ecstasy, as if just returning from a grand concert, or a beautiful garden filled with music, color, and perfume, and a peculiar feeling akin to what I would imagine is caused by opium or morphine, as nearly as I could understand it. Once felt, it is always craved. But whereas drugs destroy in reaction, this seemed to strengthen, giving greater endurance, greater power, greater precision and command to all activity, both of body and mind. This is the "Feeling" (with a capital F).

There is a less pronounced sensation involved in so-called thought transference. I say "so-called" since in reality no thought, as we ordinarily consider thought, is transferred at all. Any thought that I experience originates in my own anatomy and not that of anyone else. I can, however, be caused to think a thought similar to the one that someone else has thought, is thinking, or will think. And in the same manner, whole masses of people can be caused to think similar or parallel thoughts.

There is only one way I know of to describe it to another who has not felt it—the feeling that distinguishes a thought thus induced (thought induction rather than thought transference), and that is to take him in a car along a street he has never seen before. I cause him to lose his sense of direction, and then ask him to check up on his sense of orientation. I ask him to make himself believe that he is going north, say, toward his home. Then I ask him to change the direction mentally, and imagine himself going south. He feels himself denying a supposed fact, and acquires the new viewpoint only after he has wiped his mental slate clean by an effort to eliminate his previous thought or belief. In so doing, he experiences a mental "sensation" that is akin to that experienced when a thought is induced by the transfer of a feeling—not of a "thought."

The acceptance and recognition of mental activity thus not self-originated, requires the voluntary or involuntary elimination of previous or present self-originated mental activity. In other terms, you must stop thinking in order to allow thought to be "induced" from external influences. But whether your mental activity is the result of current direct from your own batteries, or current induced by the activity of your sympathetic nervous system in response to external influences, it is nevertheless still your own memory elements that are stimulated to constitute your "thought." Therefore the term *thought transference* is a misleading one, involving a conception that is not in accordance with human experience and experiment.

Chapter IV

As a young man I began to visit all the various denominations of churches in the city, and to investigate all forms of religious belief and worship. There were many questions I wished to ask, but hesitated to state because I did not want to appear unduly inquisitive. I soon discovered, however, that if I asked these questions "mentally," in my own mind, without putting them in words, I would receive the answer in one way or another, during a conversation or discourse of the ministers or speakers.

I experimented with this for a while, without anyone knowing what I was doing. I received such strange and direct answers to my mental questions that I was led to experiment in having others ask silent questions of me.

The procedure was to start a conversation with the understanding that my questioner was only to think his questions, to talk about anything he pleased, but never to state the question he wished answered. Afterward we would compare notes, and I discovered that it was often easier to answer these unspoken questions than it was to answer questions put directly into words. Moreover, my answers to nine out of every ten questions were correct. What was functioning here?

In the first place, not knowing the question, my part of the conversation was spontaneous and without constraint or concentration of effort, as was the case when faced with a direct question that I was expected to answer in the same direct manner.

In the second place, at no time did I make an effort to discover what the question was, either by questions on my part, or an effort to "sense" it or "read the mind" of my questioner. I refrained from this for the simple reason that when I tried it, I was obliged to "think about it," and my best chance of success was not to think about it at all.

Consequently I never knew when or if I had answered the question until it came time to compare notes on the result. I would say or talk about whatever popped up in my mind during the conversation. More often than not it was something entirely foreign to the conversation, and consequently more often than not, I really didn't know what I was talking about at all.

This was the origin of a deliberate effort on my part to apply the principle of "effortless thought without thinking" on an experimental basis.

The result of these early experiments, however, gradually got me deeper and deeper into a situation from which I was later able to extricate myself only by the drastic means of leaving the city and seeking seclusion. Word got around all too quickly that all a person had to do to get the answers to all his problems and troubles was to have a little talk with me.

At first, I was glad enough to have people come to me, without my having to go to them, to carry on my experiment. It gave me a chance to learn a lot about human nature, human thinking, and the troubles and problems of the people at large. Moreover, it gave me a chance to practice and further develop the rather unusual art of "talking without thinking." Now, instead of being obliged to depend entirely on "images," I began to gain a greater facility in drawing on "words" in response to my "feelings."

But the less fortunate side of this experience, so far as I was concerned, was that as many as one hundred people per day, often more than that, would come to the place where I lived. This began to consume all my strength and time, so that it was difficult to earn a livelihood—and I would not "commercialize" what I felt should be held "without money and without price." Further, many of the people who came to me were poor and in need, with real trouble and problems of life beyond their capacity to solve them for themselves.

Also, the main requirement for my success in helping them was a sensitive, sympathetic attitude on my part, to which I submitted to such extent that their troubles were my troubles. I became bound to them. I could not refuse them what comfort I could give. And I shall never attempt to describe what I suffered as a consequence of this, sweating with them, shedding tears with and for them, keeping my nerves almost raw so that I would not fail them, praying for help, if help could be had from any "higher power," so I could meet these demands.

From a casual experiment I was plunged over my head into the midst of human woes, with people by the hundreds looking to me to relieve them from those woes, in a world where war had taken toll again, and where charlatans had risen by the score, of all types, to deceive them.

And still further, advantage was taken of me at every turn. Many came to me out of curiosity alone. I had not then developed resistance to this, and did not like to offend. So when businessmen came to me with their trouble, I was often drawn into considerations with regard to which I was not prepared by experience to understand the real issues involved.

For example, as the time drew near for another presidential election in 1900, William McKinley was nominated for re-election on the Republican ticket, with Theodore Roosevelt, then governor of New York, as vice president. William Jennings Bryan was nominated for president on the Democratic ticket, and there were a number of other minor parties, each with a candidate for president.

For a reason I did not at first understand, the outcome of this election was considered to be "crucial" by many businessmen, officials of various corporations, and one in particular (within the circle of my "friends and their friends"), J.W.A., who was a member of the board of Trade In Chicago. The subject came up continually in conversations as the elections drew near and for the first time in my experience, I found myself being drawn outside of purely personal considerations into the whirlpool of national politics and affairs.

For the first time, too, I found myself wondering about these things. For this would be my first experience in voting as a citizen of the United States. At the time of McKinley's first election in 1896 I had been only nineteen years old, and it was only in 1898 that I attained my majority of derivative citizenship due to the naturalization of my father before his death, when I was a minor.

So now I took the matter of voting seriously, and wanted to know whom to vote for, and why. But the issues of the election were confusing. From all I knew previous to that time, they should have depended largely on questions of principle and policy in dealing with the colonial possessions that were taken from Spain in the Spanish-American War. There were questions of believing in war or not believing in war, of the liberties and treatment of peoples, of the principles of democracy, the spirit of the Constitution of the United States, and American ideals in general.

But now there was talk of a monetary question again. That had been an issue in the 1896 election. The Democratic party had sought to introduce a silver standard, and the Republican party, taking a stand for the gold standard, had won out. The result of this election in subsequent legislation should have settled the matter, and everyone thought it was settled. Even the Democratic party was willing to regard it as settled and concede their cause as "lost." But Mr. Bryan, as the Democratic nominee, insisted on raising the issue again. As a result of this, there was an unexpected confusion in the minds of those who took their responsibilities of citizenship seriously.

Many who favored Mr. Bryan's views against militarism and existing colonial policies, and who were also in favor of his concept of a Christian Americanism, could not, for practical and economic reasons affecting their private interests, favor his proposal for a silver monetary standard.

Many who felt it necessary to support the Republican view in regard to the gold standard did not approve of what they called "the greedy commercialism" that dictated the Philippine policy of the Republican administration.

The result was that there were many in both parties who could not wholly approve of either candidate. As a consequence of this there was great apprehension in the commercial and industrial world with regard to the probable outcome of the election. And into this confusion of issues and uneasiness of spirit I was drawn through the instrumentality of friends and those who sought to take advantage of my mental experiments.

??? What immunity I might have had through my own concern as to how I should vote in this, my first election, though I had nothing personally at stake, no matter what the outcome might be. In the first place, I was aware that this time, because of the confusion of issues, many would not vote at all. I considered doing the same myself, but then I reflected that it would not be a good way to start my career as a citizen. I asked myself the question, "*Is the majority always right? Do the people make the best choice?*"

Suddenly I discovered that I wanted to know who was going to be elected. I had never asked myself such a question before, as a mental experiment. But now I did, I "blanked" my mind and turned my imagination loose to catch the answer from my "feeling." The result was a mental flash of a newspaper headline bearing the name of McKinley and containing a figure somewhat in excess of half a million majority. So I felt that while I was in no position to judge the issues on the little knowledge I then possessed, I would assume that the majority were right, and vote for McKinley.

If that had been all, this book would probably never have been written, and the whole future course of my life and thoughts would have been changed. But it was not all. In the course of my conversation with a number of businessmen, including the above-mentioned J.W.A., when they asked me questions concerning the coming election, I forthwith answered now what I had never been able to "feel" in their presence, that I thought McKinley would be elected by about half a million majority.

I do not recall any special reaction to these conversations except in the case of J.W.A. Upon that occasion, however, I experienced a phenomenon that was new in my life. After predicting to him the outcome of the forthcoming election, I became suddenly confused, and felt a sense of panic and shock, followed by such a feeling of depletion, shame, and dejection that I thought I was going to be ill. I could not comprehend it. It was as if a light in my heart and mind had suddenly been extinguished, leaving me in darkness. The "feeling" I had come to regard as an ever-present function, as much "mine" as my sense of sight or hearing, left me. From that moment I was unable to "feel" or sense anything. I could only reason things out. My intuition had died a sudden death. Why?

I cannot hope to describe the feeling of desolation that came over me. People came to me with their troubles, and I could only sympathize with them by common sense and reason. I walked the streets so people would not find me home. I went out alone at night under the stars to shed tears where none could see me, and to pray and sweat it out alone to find the answer. Why? *Why?*

The election came and went. McKinley won by a little over 800,000 majority. I bought a copy of the paper with the headlines I had "seen" in answer to my mental query that had somehow betrayed me. Then I found that Mr. J.W.A., as a member of the Board of Trade, had cashed in on my prediction to an extent that netted him a profit of one hundred and fifty thousand dollars or more.

What was the answer? As days went into weeks, weeks into months, I was to ask myself that question a thousand times, until I had written the answer so deeply that it was never to be forgotten.

There was only one answer, and I couldn't squirm out of it, no matter how I tried to reason it out. My eyes and ears were mine to use or misuse at will. But the *feeling* was a *gift* that I was not free to misuse without suffering the penalty of losing it. Perhaps there was some natural law I did not understand, and which I had unknowingly violated. Perhaps it was an operation of a "spirit of truth" or intelligence, such as the Bible described.

In any case, whatever I had believed as a child, whatever I might now assume from a rational standpoint, coincident with "coming of age" as an adult citizen of these United States, I was painfully faced with the fact that my nervous system had sustained a relationship with some unknown "source" of inspirational energy that operated only on conditions, and that I was still largely ignorant of those conditions, and that as a child I had not been expected to know those conditions, but that now as an adult I was responsible for the violation of those conditions—even through the instrumentality of others. Ignorance of the law appeared to be no excuse.

The whole affair appeared to originate in my conversation with J.W.A. Whatever the fault, I was to blame, not he. I did not receive one penny from him as a result of his profits from my prediction, yet I was paying the price for it. And he never knew nor could he have understood the price I paid.

Other men had profited in one way or another from the by-products of my mental experiments, but not to this extent. Then why, in principle, make an issue of this case? Was it because I had given away without discrimination what had been given me in private as an answer to my own question, asked for a very different reason?

In any case, here I was with only logic and reason left to me, forced to conclusions against which my logic and reason revolted. What I had regarded as a physiological operation of my nervous system, which involved "feelings" as tangible as those of heat and cold and electrical currents, had proved to depend only in a secondary sense on the physiological and nervous mechanism I possessed. Primarily it depended upon the operation or co-operation of something "other than myself," and I was undergoing a reluctant proof of this fact by having the primary "current" shut off. My prayers and tears and torture were of no avail. I had to think my own thoughts. The thrill of having them induced by inspiration was mine no more.

It was then that I knew what made charlatans and fraudulent spiritists, even granting that they had possessed some kind of gift. For if and when they lost it for any reason at all, they were obliged to go on by "pretending." Because they commercialized it, their livelihood depended on it, and when it failed them, they substituted tricks.

It became evident to me that there was some kind of spiritual ethics that was not very well understood. So I made up my mind that I would prepare myself with a better foundation for making use of intuition, if I should ever succeed in regaining what I had lost. And this included insuring my own future freedom and independence, with a means of livelihood that would not be incompatible with a continuation of my research, though not dependent on it from a psychological angle.

To this end I went to work at any job I could find. I spent all the money I could spare on instruments and apparatus, and all my spare time familiarizing myself by experiment rather than textbooks with the principles of electricity, chemistry, and microscopy. I bought the finest microscope that I could obtain at that time, and because it was a better one than any of my doctor friends possessed, I worked with them evenings in return for specimen. Thus I started my studies of biology and physiology, having made up my mind that if the gates of my mind were going to stay closed, I would take up medicine and become a doctor.

But I did not fix my mind too strongly on this thought, because I still had the vision of workshops and a research laboratory, where, if my intuition did not fail me altogether, I would delve into the mysteries of nature that constituted the still unsolved problems of science and support this dream of pure research by an occasional invention of a practical kind.

Thus ended the first twenty-three years of my life, with the loss of the "feeling" that had led me through all, from childhood.

Exactly one year to the day from the time my "feeling" left me, it returned again, just as if an electrical switch, long disconnected, was again turned on.

What this exactitude of period might mean I did not then know. It was as if I had been sentenced to one year in "jail," a jail with only two windows, my eyes, and all the other gates of my mind barred shut. For though I could hear, what I heard meant little. And though I could still smell the odor of flowers in spring, the experience stirred no response. The flavor of food gave me no pleasure. My appetite was gone. Things that I touched were cold or warm, rough or smooth, but I could not feel them a part of me, to interpret their hidden meanings as I had done since childhood. My imagination and emotions, which had previously been ever active, sensitive to respond, were during this year entirely dormant.

For the first time I felt the deficiency of my education, for now what had been the source of my understanding was no longer active. I felt that I knew nothing whatever about anything at all. So I set out to learn what I could while working for a living, along with thousands of others who were serving "sentences" longer and harder than mine, in the endless treadmill of the civilization of a large city.

The story of that year would be superfluous to this record. Suffice to say that in that time I was reduced to the humility of realizing that "in myself I am nothing," and that other men in themselves were nothing—that without inspiration, all men were nothing but electrochemical, biophysical mechanisms.

Then what was inspiration? What was the "current," and from whence, that brought life to dormant nerves, vision and understanding to the mind? I could see that men did not realize. The blind followed the blind, and none of them knew.

What made men great musicians, great artists, poets, surgeons, scientists, leaders, prophets? Was it the men themselves? What and whence the energy, the enthusiasm, the ambition, the hope and faith, the vision that took the clay of the earth, the body of an animal, and raised up out of the mob a great and lonely man?

And why did men flourish for a season, rise up inspired and speak their piece to thrill a nation, only to sink back to the level of a beast again, with a glaze over their eyes, a palsied hand, a pathetic ghost of a once-great man?

Only now did I know the answer, in the only way that one can ever know the answer to anything, by a personal experience. My little light hadn't lit up a very large area. It was the light of a boy, not a leader. I was not a great musician, artist, or anything else. Comparatively few people even knew I existed. But my light had gone out. And I could see in the lives of other men that they too had flashed a greater light than mine, but it had gone out.

We were the wires and the bulb, the machine and the motor, but without the "current" we were nothing but that. It required a man plus "something else." Without the man, the "something else" could not manifest. Without the man the "something else" would be without hands, without voice, without strings to play a melody. But conversely, without that "something else" men are but the clay of the earth, and go the way of all flesh as a herd of educated human animals. And I could see that if man did not sustain a proper relation with that "something else," it left him as quickly as the snapping off of a switch or the burning out of a light.

Further I could see that it was this "something else" that had been responsible for all scientific progress. Yet still the scientists could only dissect the mechanism, trace the circuits of the nerves, and experiment with the functions and disorders of the organs. But science had not yet detected the function in its own progress of that "something else" that caused even the hearts of scientists to burn with the thrill of great discoveries, which they ignorantly presumed themselves to be making because they rightly assumed that their thoughts and conclusions consisted of happy correlations of their own observations, experiments, and sensory experience. But they wrongly ignored the function of the very energy that animated them in the fusion of their memories as an activity of understanding, failing to realize that without this inspiration they could not have been led to make the discovery, that it was not "accidental," as they thought, and that were it not for the "something else," they would have gone the way of all the uninspired on the endless treadmill of the world's repetition of routine.

And still further I could see that religion had developed a vocabulary with which to do a lot of talking and preaching about this "something else," which had shown what it could do with men now dead for centuries, but seemed careful not to imply too strongly or to encourage the expectations that even granting the omnipotence of that "something else" it can do the same things today.

If the sun had gone out, whence the heat and life of earth and man at this moment? But with my own light out, I could understand the past tense of religions from which the light had fled — living on memories, doctrines and speculative beliefs. What else was left? What indeed could we do but cling as best we might to a lost faith that, having ceased to be operative physiologically, had become a legend, where people worshiped at an empty grave that was but a reflection of their own lives, from which the living, vibrant "something else" had fled, leaving but an echo and a "word"?

So I who had stayed outside of the churches that could not feed me with a living God, to fill every nerve with life and understanding, I who had said, "Fill me with the spirit if there is such a thing, don't talk to me about it." Now I could understand. My heart ached for us all. I, too, now lived on a memory that began to fade like an echo without a voice to sustain it.

I say all this in the hope of conveying some understanding of what it meant to be released again from the prison of my own skull, the gates of my mind flung open once more, dormant nerves alive again, so that the whole universe from which I had seemed to be a separate thing now seemed to be inside, instead of outside my head. The moon, the sun, and the stars, the trees and the people, I saw in that moment seemed to be as much a part of me as my own hands and feet.

I shook hands with a friend, and suddenly felt a pain in the lower right side of my abdomen. Not having seen him for some time I asked him how he was, and he told me he had ruptured himself lifting a heavy packing case.

I was introduced to a man and a woman, total strangers to me. When I looked at the head of the man, I imagined for an instant that it resembled a long, high bridge. When I looked at the woman, for a moment her face seemed to me to be that of an old man holding a violin under his chin. When I laughingly told them about it, the man said, "That is strange. I am working on the specifications for a new ridge over the Mississippi River. I am an engineer."

The woman said, "Why, whatever made you say that? I never heard of such a thing! I have been thinking of just such a man. I met him at a musical in Paris, and he promised to give me lessons when I returned. I am planning to go there now."

A man was brought to see me by a friend who said, "Joseph, this man has heard of your mental experiments and would like to talk with you about them."

When I shook hands with him, a feeling of cold crept up my arm like a cold draft that went all through me and chilled me from head to foot. I was hard put to complete the handshake courteously, without betraying my revulsion to the feeling.

During the meaningless formalities of opening a conversation, I kept asking myself, "Now what does that mean? What does that feeling mean?" But my mind went blank, and produced no answer. That was the answer, and I didn't know it at first.

The man said, "I thought perhaps you could tell me something of what I ought to do. I have become confused in my mind, and the doctors can't help me with it. They don't find anything wrong with me physically."

I said, "Well, I can tell you what you are going to have to do, if you don't let up a little, and take better care of yourself. You are going to have to take a long rest."

"Do you think I should quit working for a while?"

"Try it for a week," I said, "And then let's talk about it again. Take a week off at once, and just rest. Then come to see me."

But I never saw him again. My friend told me that he dropped dead at his work, having arranged to finish the week out before taking a vacation.

Thus began a long period of adjustment between myself as a physiological mechanism, of which I now had a better knowledge, and the rest of the universe in connection with which there was "something else" that appeared to be establishing a relation with my imagination and memory through the involuntary nervous system.

It was not all clear sailing, and I proceeded with a caution I had not exerted before, as I was determined both to test out its limitations, or perhaps I had better say my limitations, and still avoid losing it again.

There appeared to be a "code" or language of "feeling" combined with mental imagery by which I could learn to extend the range of my interpretation of conditions. For example, the cold draft up the arm, and the inability to imagine anything when death was near, and there was nothing that could be said or done.

Then, too, there were lessons to be learned regarding the conditions necessary to sustain a cooperative relation between the voluntary and the involuntary nervous systems. Perhaps it was well not to spend time theorizing about it, but rather merely to state a few of the facts.

Some of my friends thought I had suddenly developed a "conscience," but I had given that considerable thought, and I knew it was not what they meant by the word. Conscience to most of them was merely a matter of childhood training as to what was right or wrong, and later in life, a social conscience based on public opinion and fear of criticism, "what people would think," and so on.

On the other hand, there is a private conscience of moral arbitration that governs conduct even in solitude, on the basis of self-respect, ideals, and aspirations. With this type of conscience I was acquainted from childhood. No, what I was now experiencing was a period of systematic training (call it self-training, if you wish), in which my voluntary nervous system was obliged to place itself in submission to the involuntary nervous system for self-preservative reasons.

The bargain that *intuition* seems to drive is that it will serve you if you serve it. You must obey your intuition to cultivate it, to develop it, and to retain the use of it. This is a voluntary act. In colloquial language, you have a *hunch,* and the hunch is an involuntary experience. Whether or not you obey it is up to you. If it is a real hunch, or intuition, you will inevitably regret it if you do not. These experiences will increase in frequency if you obey them, and if you don't, they will cease altogether. This is evident from case histories.

But to complete the transaction one must go further than that. One must recondition the entire system of reflexes that constitute habit, so that neither habit, nor sensory stimuli, nor the influence or suggestions of environments, thoughts, desires, or purposes of other people can interfere with the function or execution of your intuition — of your relation between your inner self and that universal "something else." That must come before all else— "or else," in the final transaction.

???

If this had not been the case to some extent with myself previously, I would have hit the drift with my hammer at the time when it would have exploded the dynamite cartridge I didn't know was there. In that and many other cases where I was not alert to exercise any caution of intuition, I would not be here to write this record if my involuntary nervous system had not been responsive to "something else" besides my own will, knowledge, experience, or senses. My arm refused to obey. On other occasions it had done just the reverse, by making a sudden movement, to my own astonishment, to prevent an accident that I had failed to prevent by a voluntary intuitive alertness.

So now this proclivity appeared to be undergoing a period of calisthenics in a series of minor issues. I would start to smoke, and experience a feeling not to do so. If I heeded it, well and good. If not, my hand would drop or throw the match away before I could light up. I have never felt required to stop smoking, but I was definitely stopped from inhaling the smoke, limited in amount, and prevented upon occasion.

I have never been a drinker, and all my life have believed and practiced moderation in all things. Therefore an occasional drink was always in order. But now I had the occasional experience (apparently as a sort of involuntary "exercise") of having a glass in my hand, but being unable to drink it.

One day I was asked to join a group on an excursion into the country, and the prospect pleased me. A day in the country away from the city was something that I would enjoy. I had "*Yes, I would be glad to go*" already framed and on the way to my vocal cords, but it came out, "*No, I'm sorry. I can't go.*"

"Why not?"

That stumped me. There was no logical reason. I wanted to go. I couldn't answer and did not feel like making false excuses to the one who was urging me, so I merely smiled and shook my head. This met with an argument. Why did I "spoil the party," and so on. They thought me stubborn. I said I would be glad to go, that I really wanted to go, but not just then. If they would wait until the day after tomorrow, I would go, but not the next day.

So the whole trip was postponed in order to have me go with them. Next day the train we would have taken was derailed in a gulley. Three were killed and many injured.

This was my wages, and countless other occasions like it, for "playing the game" that developed and conditioned involuntary reflex actions to the promptings of an intuitive feeling. If I had not allowed myself to respond to the reactions that threw a match away before I could light a smoke, and stopped my hand before it could raise a drink to my mouth, I would have been without that hand and perhaps my eyes from an explosion, and I would have said what I tried to say, "*Yes, I would be glad to go,*" and we would all have been on the train that was wrecked.

And still, it is interesting to note that in "playing the game" above mentioned, I have in the long run never been disproved of anything, but have been merely reduced to moderation in all things. First, however, I had to demonstrate a willingness to give up anything and everything, to do things I did not want to do, and to refrain from things I did want to do—all to the end of clearing the road for the *greater freedom.*

Friends have thought that I was obeying an "impulse." No, it is not that. It is an intuitive determination to follow an inspired thought. The thought is my own, an activity of my own mind and nervous system, but an activity that would not take place unless it was induced by a feeling that constitutes inspiration, and that emanates from "something else," not my own.

I have utterly failed from the viewpoint of science and psychology to be able to account for the results of experiments in field or laboratory without that "something else." I find by investigation that men who can do so on a purely mechanistic basis are themselves merely talking machines confined to the electrical recordings of their verbal memory. My radio is mechanistic also, but it has to have a "broadcasting station," and that is the "something else."

I confess there are no "call letters" to the human radio "station." I do not know what or who or where the "vibrations" or radiant energy comes from that is transformed into an activity of the imagination by means of selective stimulation of memory elements, but I do know that, so far as I am concerned, together with my associates through many years of research, on the basis of experience, observation, and experiment, on an operational, not a theoretical scientific, basis, we have established the fact for ourselves that man's survival and progress on a level superior to that of an intelligent animal depends entirely upon his rising above the level of a talking machine and establishing a relation as a "receiver" to "something else."

Name it what you please, it will still be the source of all inspiration, all great art, music, literature, culture, and scientific discoveries. And it will still be what has produced the world's scriptures and spiritual concepts. All the evidence we can deduce today, tends to establish the fact that one Jesus of Nazareth and His apostles knew what they were talking about, and that the mental activity of those who think otherwise is confined to the reflective operations of the sensory and verbal memory. This is indeed a self-sufficient "mechanism," and that only, but without any dependable relation with truth or the rest of the universe, unless it is responsive to the "something else" that has the power to shape out of the sensory and verbal memory an activity of the imagination that corresponds with or portrays not only past and present, near and distant, but also future facts.

This is something that each individual may test out for himself. It is possible for any and every human being to "prophesy," if he will fulfill the conditions. The survival of our Christian civilization depends on it. It cannot survive on the basis of doctrinal beliefs, or a legendary, speculative faith. It must be an operative faith, rooted in a physiological inspiration of prophetic intuition that will restore to mankind his heritage of spiritual gifts.

This is the inner nature of the present historic crisis, and I foresaw this crisis and described it more than fifty years ago. The survival of our Christian-American civilization and democratic way of life depends on it. Christianity will survive, but not the speculative churches, and not our democratic way of life, unless history is supplemented by prophecy, and unless a doctrinal God is supplanted by a living God, and a phenomenal "something else" that can enter our lives through our nervous system on a basis at least equal to that of the radio broadcasting that now perpetually enters our ears.

I have for half a century since the early period that serves the purpose of this commentary lived my life to discover, to prove, and to exemplify this truth, and the conditions that make such a relation possible. But that is still another story. And it includes the finding of Mary Lillian, the building of my home and laboratories in the Valley of the Pines, the birth of my sons, and the records of my search and research for the truths we understand and live by.

[FIRST EDITION ENDED HERE]

Chapter V

I felt that the time had come to sink roots and grow the tree that might provide shade and shelter and fruit for those who sought what I had found. My unspoken prayer was "Show me the way, and I will follow it."

Then, as in a dream, I saw a road stretch out before me. It entered a city but did not end there. It led to the shore of a large body of water. Over the water I saw a tiny finger of light, like the beacon of a lighthouse coming from the opposite shore.

In my imagination it seemed that all I need do was to look and think in order to acquire the power of locomotion in the direction of my gaze. So I imagined myself flying, as a sea gull, out over the water, drawn onward by that beacon of light.

As I neared the other shore, in this evening flight of imagination, I saw a little stream that the light illuminated. From a small inland lake this stream ran parallel with the shore through a pond into a shallow valley between a hillside of timber on the left, and more gently sloping hills of pastureland on the right.

I made a diagram of this visionary valley in my notebook, and wrote beneath it, "This is my valley. I am now going home."

Then I set out in search of it. I did not doubt for a moment that it existed. But I did not immediately find it. I went to California to meet friends who were to return east with me. We climbed to the top of one of the Hollywood hills, where we put up a large wooden cross as a landmark.

I looked down and said to my companions, "Someday I am coming back here again, and even now I can see how it will look then. All that we see from here will be filled with streets and building, homes, streetcars. And at night it will be ablaze with lights like the reflection of stars in a mirror. We could stay here and become a part of all that progress. We could own land here and become wealthy. But at what price? Are we to be as other men? Or shall we do what other men have never thought of doing, and discover things they little dream exist?"

I knew then that this was not the hillside of my vision. I knew that the valley of my dream must remain un-desecrated by the world for another half a century.

It was Valentine's Day, and I had promised to spend the evening with Mother at the home of my sister Bertha and her family. They had built an apartment building and lived in one of the apartments, on the second floor. A few friends were expected to join us.

As I stood outside before going in, I saw someone in the lower apartment. I caught just a glimpse of a pair of large, dark, calm eyes beneath a clear, white brow. It was the face of a girl prematurely poised, like the portrait of a virgin newly emerged from the chrysalis of a childhood that lingered still like haunting, half-forgotten memories.

I thought: Where have I seen her before? But no answer was forthcoming, save that I had never seen her before. No such person had been in the neighborhood before I had gone west.

I shrugged to myself and dismissed the thought. But it was not to be dismissed so easily. Those dark eyes haunted me. Moreover, they seemed to challenge me, and I could not define why.

I thought: How deceiving their calmness, like the surface of two deep pools in the starlight. What fire, what pride, what depths of hurt or loyalty were hidden there?

A little later, when I was upstairs, I asked my mother, "Who lives below here?"

She said, "A young friend of mine and her mother. She visits with me often, and we sew together. I have been telling her about you, Joseph. I want you to meet her and talk with her. She is such a fine, sweet girl, much too young to be working all day every day helping to support her mother, and working at home besides. She does not have the social life that she has been accustomed to, and that she should be having right now. Perhaps you can help her and advise what she ought to do. She would not ask it. She is too proud for that. But you will do this for me?"

"How old is she, Mother?"

"She is sixteen or seventeen, but you would think she was older by her actions. She has the poise of twenty, and a quiet determination that exceeds mine. I often wonder at the nimbleness of her fingers and the things she is able to do so quickly and quietly that you hardly know she has done them."

"You have not yet told me her name, Mother."

"Haven't I, Joseph? Well, it is Lillian. I shall ask Bertha to invite her up here this very evening, if she will come, and you will see for yourself what I mean."

So for Mother's sake—and for absolutely no other reason—I found myself facing a slim, dark-haired little lady whose proud but graceful carriage and long, black eyelashes might have stepped out of the family portrait of a southern cavalier planter and his children before the Civil War.

From her black eyes, so clam, so poised, so indifferent at first, there now sparkled a flash of mingled amusement and defiance.

I exclaimed, "But your name should have been Mary!"

"Well," she admitted, "my full name is Mary Lillian."

"Then what are you doing this far north?" I asked her. "You are a southern girl, or I'll never make another guess about anything."

"Yes, that is true. I was born and reared in Kentucky, but now I live in Chicago. I don't see what my name has to do with that. There are lots of Marys in the North."

I laughed. "Of course that's true. But I felt you were a southern girl at the same time I knew from your eyes that your name should be Mary. If one was right, I knew the other was right—and something else besides. You didn't want to talk with me, did you?"

At this she smiled, and said, "Well, I didn't believe all they told me."

I said, "I hope you didn't!"

She added, smiling quizzically, "Because if it were all true—well, it just couldn't be true, that's all. No one could know things like they say you do. And if they did, I would not want to know them. Imagine how I would feel right now if I thought you could know all my past, and what I am thinking, and what is going to become of me!"

I said, "If I tell you the truth about all that, will you keep it a secret?"

Surprised and suddenly serious, she said, "Certainly. I will not mention anything you tell me, but I do not ask you to tell me anything."

"Well, the truth is that I don't know any of the things people think I do. If I told you all about your past, I would not know what I was talking about. I might sense your thoughts, but I don't try and I don't pry. If it is given to me to see a vision for your future, it is not I, for I have no such vision of myself. I am only a little messenger boy delivering a wireless telegram. I don't even open it to read it, and try to remember it and understand it myself. Can you understand that?"

"I don't know. I'll have to think about it. I'll try."

"Then maybe I can help by showing you what I mean. I don't know anything of your past, but it is given me to realize by intuition that from the day of your birth up to now there has not been one single thing you have ever done or thought that you need be ashamed of. I see tears, because you have lost things in life that were dear to you.

74

Through no fault of your own you have been deprived of much that should have been yours, in home environment and advantages. Your loyalty has robbed you of girlhood days and personal advancement. As I told you, I don't know what I am talking about, but you do. Don't you?"

She looked at me with wide eyes, her breath suspended. She whispered, "Yes."

"And to show you that details are possible, though we won't go into them, what happened to one of your three rings, the one you did not bring with you?"

"Why didn't you have it repaired?"

"Because it was hardly worth it. The ring wasn't very valuable."

"Oh, but it was. You knew those were real emerald, didn't you?"

"Yes." She said. "Yes, I knew it, but I don't see how you did, since I said it wasn't valuable."

"Well, there you are," I smiled at her now. "I didn't know it. I didn't have the slightest idea that you even owned a ring, or that the stones were emeralds, until it popped out of my mouth, and I heard myself telling you about it. Do you begin to understand how it is?"

She took a deep breath, and said, "It sounds so simple when you say it, but it will take me longer than this to begin to understand how it is."

"Well, all that matters right now, Mary Lillian, is that you realize that I do not claim to know these things myself, but when they come to me, if they do, they are true. That is the only reason for mentioning things that you already know. Now I will tell you something I see that you don't know. I am only doing this so you will stop worrying like you sometimes do, without anyone knowing about it. You don't need to worry about anything in your future. About a year from now you will have a home of your own, and everything will be changed."

"You mean I will be married?"

"Yes, you will be married before that time."

"Won't I be in Chicago?"

"No, you will not be living in any city."

"Oh!" she exclaimed. "But I won't live on a farm! I've always said that I would never marry a farmer! If I had to live on a farm, I would never marry at all!"

75

"Well, I agree that you will never be a farmer's wife, but you will live in the country. It will not be a farm, exactly, but a beauty spot, with woods and a stream, near a lake. You will have flower gardens all about, and if there is any farming it will be only a kitchen garden for your own use, with pasture for cows and horses, so that you will have fresh milk and riding horses. Of course, you will visit the city from time to time, and later in life will travel. The older you get, the more beautiful you will become, and the best part of your life will come last."

After that Mary Lillian was often present of an evening in a group with her mother, my mother and sister, or a few friends. We grew to know each other, but it was a growth as intangible as that of the roots of a tree. In silence, and without even the touch of our hands, the unseen waves of understanding played between us. When the conversation of others took a turn that amused us, or bored us, or exasperated us, a brief glance at each other, a single flash of eyes, fully conveyed our view to each other. We had expressed ourselves. We had been understood. We were strengthened. We felt relieved.

With the summer ahead, I announced my intentions of going camping in Michigan. I was going to follow the little beacon light of my vision and hunt for my future home. The idea of escaping the city and camping in the woods by the waters of Michigan so appealed to our little circle of friends that when we took the boat from Chicago, on June 6, armed with tents, cots, blankets, and other equipment, we had a crew of six men, three of whom brought along their wives, and there was a woman besides who had agreed to undertake the cooking.

On the south side of White Lake we set up a small permanent camp for the season. Other friends were to come from time to time, and for varying periods, for their vacations.

Mary Lillian and her mother came over to spend the last two weeks in June with us, and there, with the wind rustling in the pines, with the water softly lapping the shore at sunset, with the fragment smoke of wood burning in our campfire, the alchemy of nature completed her binding. Yet nothing was said to reveal it. But when they left, I knew the time had come. I was so lonesome that everybody noticed it, and concluded the reason. A pall settled over the whole camp. Finally, the others all talked it over behind my back, and decided that the best thing to do was to send someone across the lake to bring Mary Lillian back again. But the moment I knew what they were planning, I put an immediate stop to it. I saw a quaint and wistful

76

vision of a little lady stepping out of the pages of history to whisper, "Why don't you speak for yourself, John?"

So I went back to the city, myself.

When Mary Lillian saw me she did not ask why I had come. I held out my hand and she placed hers within it. I said, "Come," and she followed me out into the summer evening.

Then she looked up into my eyes, and asked, "When?"

I said, "Now and forever."

We were married on July 3. Then I brought her back to camp again.

I had placed a diagram and description of the kind of place I was looking for in the hands of real-estate agents. It was not long before one of them, Frank Pryor of Montague, told me, "You know, there is such a place as you describe just north of White Lake on the Old Channel. Your description sounds just like the old Redman estate. The creek runs through it, and there's a stand of pine timber on one hillside, pastureland on the other, with a house, barn, pigsty, and woodshed. The house is nothing to brag about, but—"

"How much land is there?"

"Eighty acres."

I said, "It's mine. How much is it worth?"

"Hold on a minute," said Mr. Pryor. "I'm just telling you that there is such a place. But it's not for sale."

"Take me out to see it. I want to talk with the owner."

"But no one lives there. The owner lives in St. Paul."

"Then wire him an offer of thirty-five hundred dollars cash for it. That is all I can raise just now."

The offer was accepted. The place was ours. But it was the next March 17, St. Patrick's Day, before we arrived bag and baggage, horse and wagon, to take possession.

From the crest of the hill overlooking the valley we faced another hillside covered with a stand of nearly virgin pine timber. At the foot of the hill a little creek wound south, to the left, through marshland and groves of cedar trees into a pond or bayou, beyond which could be seen and heard the waves of Lake Michigan pounding onto shore and leaping high with outstretched arms of white spray.

There was no mistaking it. This was it. The Valley of the Pines—and the valley of my vision.

Then one day, as spring slipped into summer, Mary Lillian whispered to me, "It won't be long now. He kicks like a boy. I think we're going to have a mechanic!"

The night watch began while an electrical storm was gathering its forces. Thunder and lightning had always terrified Mary Lillian, but now there was a different look in her eyes. As the hours crept by, I could almost see the white mantel of motherhood descending upon her.

The whole house shook with reverberations of thunder, which somehow seemed determined to emphasize this night as a special event in our lives.

At ten-thirty the storm reached a climax in one terrific bolt of lightning. It struck so near the house that the sound of the concussion that nearly deafened us was simultaneous with the wake of the bright flash that lit up Mary Lillian's pale face. She caught her breath, and I thought for a moment that she was going to scream, but she did not.

I rose to go to her, but the doctor pushed me aside, because he was busy.

Joseph Junior had entered the world.

When the doctor had gone and she was resting more easily, with the baby in her arms, we looked at each other without saying a word. I reached out my hands and she understood instantly. She laid our son in my arms.

It was only a symbol, but I could not find the words to explain it. So without saying anything, I raised the child toward the ceiling as if offering it to the Most High. I heard only a murmur from Mary Lillian, but I knew that she understood me, for she whispered, "Amen!"

Somehow, as time went on, the world beat a path to our door, until we had to build a large gate across the road leading into the valley, and keep it closed except to those who came by invitation.

We never allowed much publicity, but a friend would bring or tell a friend who told a friend . . . and finally I began to receive letters from all over the country, and other countries, questioning me along the line of mental phenomena and intuition. And I, in turn, began questioning others about their views and experience, until a large correspondence became part of my research, in which I would ask others in all parts of the country to check whether there was any foundation to things that I sensed.

I used to keep track of this correspondence by sticking pins in a globe and on maps, in some seven hundred cities in forty countries. Often in the evenings or late at night, I would look at those pins and let my eye be drawn to one of them in connection with a feeling that someone was thinking of me, or that someone was ill, or dying, or in trouble. If I could sense or figure out who it was, I would write and ask them to confirm it, if that was the case.

Sometimes, too, my eye would be drawn to some other part of the map, where there were no pins, where there was no one I knew, or had ever contacted. Yet I would imagine a fire or a storm or a ship sinking, and then express this to witnesses who would watch the news to see whether I was right.

Again and again through the months, the plight of people on sinking ships, of miners trapped and doomed to death in mines, of planes out of control, of individual tragedies forced themselves unsought upon the screen of my mind. It ceased to be a problem of establishing the facts, but rather of gaining and providing a better understanding of them, so that, perhaps, some day — who knows? — there might be developed a sort of clearing house for amateur "human radios," as there now began to appear for wireless and amateur radio "hams."

Would it ever prove practical for human sensitivity to be harnessed and directed to do some good in the world, to prevent things that are sensed, or to go to the rescue of men who would die unheard and otherwise without help? Some system of sifting out false thoughts would have to be developed, so that a thousand groundless fancies need not interfere with the evaluation and function of one truly intuitive thought. If we could "pool" our intuitions, one might supplement the other, and in the strength that comes from union a great deal of good might be accomplished. But working alone, the only purpose that has been served by a great many of my own intuitions was the satisfaction of my own research and the enlightenment of a few friends.

For example, during the latter part of March 1912, Charley Abel was helping me put a star clock on a little tower we had built on the hill overlooking the Valley of the Pines. For several evenings we adjusted the clock, checking the hours in connection with the advance of the date.

One evening I began to feel excited, and wondered why. It occurred to me that if we watched closely and did not fall asleep between times, we might see a meteor. I spoke of this to Charley, and we watched for three or four hours, but nothing happened. Charley would doze off, and I would wake him, saying, "Keep awake, Charley. This is something you will never see again."

To myself I wondered why the feeling of excitement persisted over seeing a meteor. I had seen hundreds of them flash across the sky.

But never before, and never since, have we seen anything like what we saw toward midnight that very evening. From northeast to southwest, a large ball of flame (which I assumed was a meteor) shot diagonally downward toward Lake Michigan. I don't know how close it was, therefore I don't know how large it was. We heard no sound of its striking anywhere, but in passing us a crescendo of sound like high-pressure steam so thoroughly startled us that we just could not take it standing up. Both of us sank down on the platform, perhaps instinctively seeking protection behind the flimsy rails that were but toothpicks, had we stopped to think.

Later, while still looking at the stars and talking about it, Charley wanted to know how I knew we were going to see a thing like that.

I answered, "I didn't."

He said, "But you told me to watch for it."

"Yes, but I didn't know it would be like that. I only felt that something was going to happen."

"What made you feel that way?"

What we were doing, I guess, working on this clock and watching the stars. We were looking north. Now when I look south, it is different."

"Yes. It's warmer, isn't it? It's pretty cold up here still. Looking south makes me feel warmer, even thinking about it."

I said, "You stop too soon. When I look south feeling cold like this, it makes me think of men freezing to death in the Antarctic. But there you are. If we weren't standing here, I wouldn't be thinking of it. So what makes one think of anything? Just because we are talking about it now, I can feel the thoughts of a man in a little tent in the Antarctic. He is dying, and he has no fuel or food. He's trying to write, but can hardly hold the pencil in his hand. He has been badly disappointed, and now he feels entirely hopeless. He has been to the pole, but someone got there ahead of him. There were dog tracks and a tent with letters in it."

Charley asked, "Is he all alone?"

I said, "I think there were five in all, but now only three are left. They are all wrapped up in some kind of sleeping bags. They don't much care what happens to them. They feel that they have suffered and sacrificed for nothing."

Suddenly, I felt horribly depressed, and said, "Oh, it's too bad! Only one of them is left alive right now. The other two are dead, and he knows it. He could save himself, but he really doesn't care. He

80

knows it is the end, and does not fear it, but he is heartsick. He keeps on writing, and I feel a pain in my kidneys and bladder when I think of him. He knows that only a few miles away is warmth and safety. He wonders if anyone can know his thoughts, and the reason he wonders is because he senses that someone does."

All of this made me feel so bad that I could not bear to think of it any longer. I did not then have any idea who the man was, but my heart went out to the man whose last thoughts were of those he loved, and of things he was too much of a gentleman to write about, of disagreement among his men that was aggravated by their disappointment, of a useless struggle. It was all so depressing that a man would not have the resistance that would save him.

This was the beginning of my interest in polar research. We did not yet have a radio, and I was not familiar with the news of world's explorations. I did not know for several months that all this was really true, and that the name of the man was Captain Scott, or that Amundsen had reached the Pole ahead of him.

But that very night I did tell the rest of my Valley, who bear witness to it, of this experience. I told them that there had been too much needless sacrifice in polar exploration.

I said, "But it will not be allowed to go on. Scientific developments will enable men to fly over the poles in safety, and they will be able to rescue men who call for help by wireless telephones. There will be no need for more lives to be lost in polar research."

For a while, my secretary Clarence Christian worked for George Mason, Sr., as office manager of the Montague Iron works. Mr. Mason became a very good friend, and I began to feel anxious about his health.

One day I told him that if he did not take a rest within three weeks, he would be forced to go to bed, and perhaps never get out of it again. But he could not see his way clear to abandon his work for a vacation, so he ended up at the hospital in Muskegon.

During this time Clarence carried on his work for Mr. Mason, and stayed at his home. One day, Clarence became so nervous he asked me to stay with him. As I entered the parlor in Mr. Mason's home, I said, "Clarence, listen to this peculiar music that comes to my mind."

I sat at the piano and played what I heard in my mind. It was so solemn and sad that it affected both of us. Then suddenly I realized that I was playing a funeral march. I imagined seeing a coffin and the remains of George Mason. My eyes filled with tears, and when Clarence asked me what was the matter, I told him.

A few mornings later I was notified that if I did not come to see Mr. Mason before noon, I would not be able to see him alive. It was impossible for me to get there in the morning, because it was already past train time. I told Clarence, "George Mason shall live till I see him. He cannot die. He shall not die."

I did not "pray" that he might live. I "willed" him to live until I might see him once more. Perhaps my assurance was based on a feeling that he would. Perhaps he would have lived until afternoon, in any case. But in all probability George Mason himself had something to do with it. For when Clarence and Charley and I arrived at the hospital, at three forty-five that afternoon, he clasped my hand, and said, "I can go, now that you have come."

My vision and the music that I had played on the piano in Mr. Mason's living room were materialized at the funeral.

For some time previous to the illness of George Mason, the large iron safe in his office had not been locked fully. The tumblers had not been thrown over. But one night after his death, Mr. Mason's son accidentally closed and locked the safe. It was then realized that no one but George Mason, Sr., had known the combination. His personal papers pertaining to the estate were in the safe, and it was now necessary that it be opened. As office manager and acting secretary, Clarence made every effort to open the safe, but without success. As a last resort, before breaking the lock, Clarence asked me to try to open it.

This was the kind of spontaneous necessity that I was always watching for as a basis for experiment. If George Mason had asked me, while living, to see if I could open his safe "just for fun," in order to see whether or not I could do it, I would not have tried it, and would not have expected to succeed if I had, unless I should sandpaper my fingers and try it as an exercise in safecracking, But with Mr. Mason dead, with no one else knowing the combination, and with the pressing need that it be opened, ideal conditions were set up for a real experiment.

I took off my hat and coat and sat at Mr. Mason's desk, just as he had always done, bending over an open ledger. I asked Clarence to blindfold me so that I would not be distracted by sight or by muscular effort to hold my eyes closed. I asked him to wait long enough for me to fully think myself into George Mason's personality, then, while I was pretending to be Mr. Mason, suddenly to ask me to open the safe.

This Clarence did, and scarcely knowing what I was doing, I turned to the safe and, to his astonishment and mine, opened it in about ten seconds. But I still did not know the combination, and immediately afterward could not have done it again with my eyes open.

Chapter VI

One day in the presence of fifteen people I began to fear that one or more of them would be in danger of drowning if they were not careful. I wanted to warn them, and in so doing found myself saying more that I had expected to say.

I said that there would be five deaths from drowning in White Lake that season—first two, then three. I asked them all please to be careful, so that none of them would be included. But Dr. Montague and a woman were drowned. That was two. Then the rest of the season passed without mishap, and I assumed with the rest that I had been wrong about the five.

One evening I took Mary Lillian and the children to Montague to attend a birthday party at the home of Joe Apoll. Joe was the one whom I had warned to be careful not to be under anything heavy supported by a chain hoist, for I had had a "daydream" of him in just such a position, and had "seen" a mental close-up of a link of the chain that would break. He did remember my warning when he actually found himself in just such a position, and stepped back, but the link broke and Joe's hand was crushed. He phoned me from the doctor's office and said, "Well, I've got it." And I still have the broken link and an X-ray picture that I took of Joe's hand.

When we arrived for the birthday party, I was told that Joseph Hazeltine had promised to come there to meet me for the first time, but he had been called out on duty as deputy sheriff at the last moment. I was told later that he had been nervous, and had said that he would "much rather have met Mr. Sadony."

At midnight or shortly after, I began to feel very nervous and depressed. I went to the graphophone and played "Nearer, My God, to Thee," which to some of those present seemed a strange thing for me to select at that stage of a birthday party. But as I looked around at the party, it began to take on the aspect in my mind of a funeral. I began to feel bad, but said nothing. I did not know how to interpret my feeling.

About two in the morning we left for home. As we passed along the shore of White Lake, I looked at the rough water and listened to the wind that we ourselves were bucking.

I said to Mary Lillian, "Wouldn't it be terrible to be out there on a night like this?" The feeling persisted, and I added, "What if two or three men were out there hanging on to a boat? God help them, if they are!"

Mary Lillian shuddered, and said, "But surely—who else would ever go out on a night like this?"

No one, of course—unless he had to. But Joseph Hazeltine "had to," he and two other men who had accompanied him on his duties. He was there instead of at the birthday party meeting me. Was he thinking of me? Was it a coincidence that we were talking about it, and shuddering as we passed the lake in the dark?

But there were the "three," found the next morning. Five deaths in the lake for the season. Was this another "coincidence"?

However, as I had never met Mr. Hazeltine, the incident did not linger long in memory at the time. So when a week later I was putting up a stovepipe, I could see no connection when a thought came to me so strongly that I stopped putting up the pipe and could not finish until I had written it down: "Fanny, I was not murdered. It was an accident. Be happy. Someone will take my place in four years."

I looked at the paper and thought, "But what has that to do with me? Why should I write a thing like that?"

Then something within me seemed to urge, "Sign your name to it." So I signed it "Joe." Still, it meant nothing to me, and I put it away.

Two months later, Mrs. Apoll visited us with a friend. She introduced her as Mrs. Fanny Hazeltine. Instantly everything connected in my mind. It was her husband, Joe Hazeltine, who had wanted to meet me, and who had been drowned instead. Now I realized that she always felt he might have been murdered. I got out what I had written her two months before, without knowing who "Fanny" was.

Mrs. Hazeltine wept when she read it, and swore that she would never marry again.

I said, 'Oh, but you will. And his name will be Joe too!"

Everybody connected with this affair seemed to be named Joe. Another "coincidence," of course. Because four years later she married again and was very happy. Her husband's name was Joe.

But was it a coincidence that I felt impelled to write, and to say what I did? Is life and everything in it a "coincidence"?

One day while I was writing a letter I heard (or thought I heard) a distinct knock at my door. After a moment of reflection and no further sound, I concluded that a blue jay or a woodpecker had been pecking at the window, and continued with my letter.

A few moments later the sound was repeated. This time there were three distinct knocks at my door. For confirmation I glanced at my dog. He did not stir, as he surely would have done, had there really been a knock.

Yet I had "heard" a knock. So I concluded that my ear must have reflected the memory of a knock in response to some "thought." I determined to test this idea. Who might want to communicate with me by "mental radio"? For the first time in a long while I thought of my father, so I turned over the reign of my imagination to his memory, and proceeded to act out my part in all seriousness.

I went to the door, opened it, let in an afternoon sunbeam, and pretended that it was my father. I said, "Well, Dad, I'm glad you have come. Sit down with me for a while. Is there something I can do for you?"

Then I took my pad and pencil and wrote down what I imagined my father was saying: "Joseph, it is three o'clock in the afternoon of August first. I wish you would build Mother a little nest of three rooms overlooking your valley, so that she may be happy there the last sixteen years of her life. Then I will come and take her with me."

I said, "Okay, Dad, I'll start today."

"Thank you, Joseph. I'll come again."

Then I snapped myself out of what seemed like a bit of idle imagining, and went back to finish my letter.

When I came to clear my desk and throw my notes and a bit of doodling into the basket, I could not leave the room. I rescued the notes of my imaginary conversation from the waste basket and phoned down for Charley to hitch up the team and be ready to help me, because I was going to haul enough gravel and sand out of Lake Michigan (about two blocks away) to make concrete blocks for a three-room house as a Christmas present for Mother, who was still living at East Lansing with Cristina and Bert King.

Charley and the rest thought that we couldn't do it by Christmas, but I was determined to try, and Mary Lillian was determined to help me. She even climbed up on the roof with me, two days before Christmas, and we finished shingling it in a snowstorm.

Mother knew nothing about all this, but next day she came from East Lansing unexpectedly to visit us. We gave our two small sons a gilded key and told them to show grandma her Christmas present.

The inside was ready for her, all lit up, a goose in the oven—there were even books on a shelf for her to read. When she saw it she

86

fainted. And when I had revived her, I asked her why she felt that way about it.

She said, "Oh, Joseph, you should not have done it!"

"But why, Mother? What makes you say that?"

"Because you can hardly afford it yet, Joseph. And I am responsible for it. One afternoon I went to church and prayed. It was like a complaint. I prayed, thinking that if only your father were here, he would build me a little nest of three rooms that I could call my own. That was all I wanted. And now you have done it."

"When was that, Mother? When did you do that?" She thought a moment, then said, "It was on August first, your Joseph's birthday."

"Was it in the afternoon?"

"Yes. About three o'clock."

I said, "Well, Mother, maybe Dad is around here, after all.

The intuitive life is not without suffering, but the suffering is that of sensitive nerves exacerbated by discord or tragedy, among other causes. For in order to carry this experiment as far as I did, you must be able to sensitize your nerves and mental clearing house so that the least sound, even that of a pin dropping on a sheet of paper, shocks you as much as an explosion, and nothing less will shock a positive man of intellect who becomes calloused and deaf to all but his objective senses.

I found that at no time was intuition more alive and active than when body and mind were either wholly absorbed and coordinated in creative labor, or exhausted with fatigue. In the first case, the intellect of reason and memory were too busy to interfere with intuition, and in the second case, too tired to do so. Therefore I kept pads of paper and pencils everywhere—in boats, in cars, in ships, by every chair where I was likely to rest, and by the side of my bed.

I made it a rule that intuition came first, before any and all other considerations, and that I would always write it down if it was not something that I could immediately execute. If my hammer was raised in the air to strike a blow, or a forkful of food on the way to my mouth at table when a thought was induced by an intuitive feeling, the nail was not to be hit by the hammer, or the food was not to reach my mouth, before I had procured pad and pencil to record it. I stood guard at the "wireless" receiver of my brain night and day, save when unconscious from sleep or sheer exhaustion—and even then, could not escape the position I had assumed.

I would wake up out of a deep sleep to find myself reaching for pad and pencil, and on many occasions in the morning found things written there that I had absolutely no recollection of writing. More than five million words accumulated in this way. I did not "think out" one word of it, and was often hard put to comprehend what my hand had written. But it was definitely not "automatic writing," so called. It was intuitive writing. The difference between the two is that between night and day.

I could fill several volumes with experiences stemming from thoughts that came to mind while working, or from the wandering of imagination when relaxed and tired after a day of hard work.

Our home would have burned down if I had not obeyed intuition one day. I sent for three large fire extinguishers at a time when running water was available, and the weather being warm, we had no fires. It was thought to be an unnecessary move just at that time, but I carefully filled them and placed them in accessible positions.

That was at eight o'clock in the evening, after supper. Exactly six hours later, at two o'clock in the morning while I was working in my shop, I looked out the window and saw flames through the window of our bedroom. A lamp had been burning there, as electricity was not at the time available. It was the first time anything like that had happened to us, and it was the first time I had ever made such deliberate and apparently unseasonal preparations for it. I had to let everything else go until I had prepared those fire extinguishers. I canceled plans to go out in the evening and stayed home quietly working in the shop, in sight of the window through which the flames were visible. But until I saw the flames, it never occurred to me to expect them. *I did not "foresee" what would happen, but I had unconsciously prepared for it.* And as time went on, I discovered that this was one of the most important aspects of the intuitive life.

I could see more clearly than ever before what the trouble was with so many people who might just as easily have avoided tragedy, as I did, not only on this occasion, but on many others. My fire extinguishers made quick shift of the blaze. We all possess a "radio" in our minds but seldom use it. Few ever learn how to use it, and many give up and cease trying when they fail.

You cannot force it. You must coax it to perform, and then accept what comes to you, even if it is nothing. It is not an "organ" that you can use at will, like our eyes. It is like radio antennae with which you may attempt to tune in, to "seek, knock and ask." Then—who knows?—you may receive a beautiful program that will illuminate and bless the rest of your life. But beware of this: if you tune in to the world of human thoughts, you shall be a slave to other men, who dominate by forceful, positive thinking.

If, however, you use your "human radio" to tune in to the Great Broadcaster of Life, you will serve the purpose of life by responding, not to the skeptical intellectual demands of men, but to those who also tuned in to the Central Broadcasting station of Mankind.

This is the foundation of human brotherhood—the brotherhood that is impossible save between intuitive men, men who know each other before they meet, and who cannot be separated even by death.

Our bodies are but the chemicals of minerals and vegetables constructed by nature to hold, to receive, and to be animated by the soul, which is that part of radiant energy we call God, a law of nature that may be symbolized by a child, chalk in hand, writing its name on a blackboard. The chalk is nature, and what it means is the child. Nature is the chalk, but God moves within. That is the Everlasting Name nature has written in its mystery.

The spirit of man is but an echo of the soul—that repeats but knows not its meaning. The spirit is the graphophone record repeating answers to problems about which it knows nothing, like my psychologist friends with their textbook knowledge—a parrot, a book, or even a prayer of mere words in a language you do not understand, though you repeat it daily for a lifetime. But let the soul express one thought, and poets will write of it for centuries.

For the soul expresses itself in whatever medium it finds available—in music, in color, in form, in the flesh of a man, in tears, in emotion, in love, in prayer—playing upon the strings of whatever instrument you are able to furnish. This is inspiration, intuition, prophetic vision. And this is what the psychologists had eliminated from their consideration, because in observing the behavior of the human graphophone machine, the human radio and television are automatically shut off.

The soul has not got a chance to "put words into your mouth" if you put them there yourself by playing the graphophone records memory, by planning and thinking what you shall do or say.

???

No, It was definitely impossible to live the intuitive life on the basis of intellectual planning. So I would apply my intuition to a

89

continued search for truth, without hope or expectation of any particular objectives or financial gain. I would concern myself with economics and industrial problems only to the extent that it was necessary to make the research possible, and thus far things have worked out all right from intuitive beginnings, without worrying about it. I began to see a practical aspect to the faith of the old (saying) that "the Lord would provide," if one obeyed the intuitions by which the Lord might find it necessary to enlist your help in so doing.

The object of my study was the mind of man. This obviously included the whole universe. Not one aspect of science, philosophy, or religion could be excluded from consideration. To establish the truth of the mind of man, I would have to build a new bridge between science and religion, for I saw that all previous attempts to do this had rested on quicksands of purely intellectual speculations.

Research in the physical sciences and in the mental sciences must proceed hand in hand on a basis of experience and experiment. One glimpse into the future staggered me. The task was more than I could do. I could only begin it. I dared not look again. I kept my eyes glued to the ground only one short step ahead. Enough that I lived today intuitively in preparation for tomorrow. Enough if I contributed one small but essential block to the structure of a new generation that would tax the skill and specialties of the world's greatest minds.

As time passed it became evident that many chains of events were unfolding here and there throughout the world, and interweaving little threads of thought that seemed to pull on my mind.

One evening, for example, I felt inclined to sit at the organ in the little chapel we had built, and improvise some music. I had spent the day in the world of intellect making a delicate magnetic instrument that I had designed for geophysical research, and before attempting to answer some of the seven or eight thousand letters that had accumulated, I felt the need to woo my way back into the world of intuition again.

I drifted into a strange melody that I had never played before. There was an oriental sadness in it, and suddenly I felt the presence or thoughts of Srikrishna Chatterjee, as if he were dead or in a coma. I had not heard from him or thought of him in a long while.

I wrote him about this and received answer that he had been at the door of death, but was now better. He informed me, however, that it had been predicted in India that he had not long to live.

In explaining my experience, I wrote him: "About the middle of February, while in my chapel, I seemed to feel your presence, just

90

as if you were in that sphere which hovers between death and life, a living dreamland, the sphere which brings me so many thoughts — as if you were in the next world, but still anchored by a silk thread to this one. I began to fear, for I felt that you had something still to complete."

As for the prediction that he had but a short time to live, I told him that I disagreed with it. In answer to it, I predicted that he would recover, make a long journey, and visit many people before his time would come.

Three years later he wrote me: "The journey was undertaken by me in October. I was seized with a desire to see my second boy and his two children and wife at Nasirabad, which must be about fifteen hundred miles from this place. I went to Calcutta, and thence proceeded. I visited Arraha, Pushkar, Chitor, Udaipur, Ujjain, and eight other places in the course of my journey."

The consequence of this journey had repercussions for me that I did not then dream about. Wherever Mr. Chatterjee went, my letter went with him. He presented himself as living testimony that the prediction of his early death (which had been made in India) was erroneous, and that my prediction for his recovery and journey, made three years before, was being fulfilled. Moreover, I had predicted that India would attain her freedom in 1948, and that by 1940 seven of her provinces would already have gained emancipation. This prediction was privately made, but it spread more widely than I had anticipated.

One day I was looking at a photograph of Tagore that hangs among others of my friends, in my study. I recalled Frederick Fisher's description of Tagore as a stolid mountain compared to Gandhi, who was a rushing torrent. And I was thinking of Frederick's account of a conversation that had taken place in his presence.

Tagore expressed his desire to remove all idols, saying, "If we can do without them, even the lowest can do likewise."

Gandhi replied, "No, you cannot do this. Idols are the poor man's crutches. They cannot walk without them until you supply them strong limbs of understanding."

Now I looked at Tagore's picture, thinking. "Can you do that, Rabindranath? Can you supply the poor of India with limbs of understanding strong enough to dispense with their crutches of idols?"

I imagined a sad expression coming over Tagore's face, even in the photograph, as if he was saying, "Joseph, I am only a poet. But I try also to teach with my melodies. I am not too strong, myself."

91

Then I saw a little black ribbon pinned to his picture. It was imaginary, of course. When I looked again it was gone. But every time this happened to me, I put a real black ribbon, a tiny one, where I thought I had seen one. For in every case the person in question had not lived more than six months. Five months and two weeks later, Rabindranath Tagore was gone.

What is the source of this "vision," this "signal"? What tells me that a friend is soon to pass on? More than a score of little black ribbons on photographs of friends bear silent witness without explaining a thing. Among them were Ella Wheeler Wilcox and Marie Corelli, Theodore Roosevelt, and, years later, his wife, Edith, with whom I corresponded until she died; Abdul Baha and Anton Lang, the Conan Doyles and Sir Oliver Lodge, Rudyard Kipling and the explorer Amundsen, General John Pershing, and Lieutenant Governor Evans, Ernest Torrence and Henry B. Walthall, Ossip Gabrilowitsch and Channing Pollock, Jessie Bonstelle, Governor Chase S. Osborn, Benjamin de Casseres, Edwards Davis, and others no less important but too numerous to mention who had left the imprint of their personalities on the Valley of the Pines. When death cast its shadow before it, that too left its imprint, sometimes in advance, and sometimes in the hour.

When 1940 saw the liberation of seven provinces, and 1948 the freedom of all India, I wrote to Gandhi that the book of my vision for India was closed. My predictions of many years before had come to pass. Of the future of India I had nothing more to say, save that she must now make her own future, and he could be of far greater service living than dead. I begged him not to fast again, after India attained her freedom, for if he did so it would lead to his death, even though he was not obliged to fast unto death. I saw the black ribbon, and I saw his death in one way or another, and recorded the fact in confidential communications to a number of witnesses.

Then one day I stood looking out the window in the Valley, for a few moments indecisive, tired, uncertain what to do next, uncertain whether it was worthwhile to do anything. I thought: This is not me. This is not the way I feel. Some other 'program' has blotted out my own 'radio.'"

I wondered what it could be. I stood there, groping with my mind, just like insects I have watched groping in all directions with their antennae, searching for some recognizable environment. It seemed dim and far away, so in order to reach it I became more and more sensitive. And in that moment Mary Lillian came quietly into the room, but there was a slight click of the door latch as she opened the door. To me it was like a gunshot, and for a moment I thought I had been shot. I clutched my side and staggered. Mary Lillian ran to me, pale and frightened.

"What's the matter, honey? What is it?"

I said, "It's nothing. I was thousands of miles away, that's all. I really thought I was shot."

She said, "I'm sorry. I frightened you."

I said, "No, it was not you. That was just a coincidence. Or was it? I don't know what it is yet. Just forget it."

Later, Mary Lillian told me, "I think I know what it was now. Were you thinking of Gandhi? I've just heard about it over the radio. You went through the same thing in your mind."

Well, I cannot say that with certainty. I was not consciously thinking of Gandhi at the moment. I was still trying to identify the thoughts that distressed me. The experience brought me to earth with such a bang that I dropped the whole thing from my mind like a bad dream, and went to work in my laboratory.

But it lingered. Nothing exactly like that had happened to me before. Was it just another "coincidence"?

I wondered.

Chapter VII

When my family and I were working with Frank R. Adams in our local dramatic club, helping to put on plays, the venture culminated in building The Playhouse, in Whitehall. This was made to pay for itself in between times by renting it for other purposes; and eventually Frank installed moving-picture equipment. It became a movie theater, and for a long time my boys managed it for Frank. Usually we all went down in the car early enough to open up the theater and stayed through both shows, as one of the boys had to be on hand till the end.

No one but my family and Meredith, who assisted me in the experiment, knew why I spent night after night in the orchestra pit at the drums, adding the pianist (who was sometimes my son Arthur) in providing sound effects during the days of silent films. And no one knew why I doggedly stayed there through two shows each time.

My procedure and the reasons were simple. I watched the picture through the first performance, studying it carefully to provide the right drumming effects, and carefully noted the repertoire of emotions each play induced in the audience. I was there to see the audience, not the picture, and from my vantage point in the orchestra pit I could see without being seen, though I was making a lot of noise in order to be heard all evening.

My little research project took place during the second run of the picture. Throughout the second performance my eyes were closed. I looked neither at the picture nor at the audience. Meredith sat where he could see both the picture and the audience, and near enough to me so that we could converse in whispers when necessary. I made it a practice to try to see the picture through the eyes of the audience instead of my own, during that second performance. Having provided myself first with a memory of the picture, I then allowed the emotions of the audience, amplified by the number of people present, to recall the various scenes at the proper time.

Thus for hours, week after week, I practiced sensing the emotions of a small "mass" of people, varying from one hundred to five hundred people—emotions that were somewhat unified and coordinated by a common object of interest and concentration. So when the *Empress of Ireland* sank, for example, I was perhaps better able than another to recognize the combined emotion of a hundred people facing the certainty of death.

But when it is a prevision, what then? I felt the shadow of the *Lusitania* disaster casting itself long beforehand. I did not sense the name *Lusitania*, but described it in terms of the shock it would bring to the rest of the world. I predicted it for the first week in May 1915. I felt the emotional reaction of the public several months beforehand.

But how could such a thing possibly be known? People asked me, "How did you know?"

And how many times was I forced to repeat, "I did not know." Knowledge is of the intellect. Prophecy is not knowledge.

I don't know why such things came to me, when it did no good to anyone, and did not serve to prevent disaster.

Of far greater service was the night I had an impulse to get out the car and drive to town and back with Mary Lillian and the boys. When I told them to get on their things, they said, "Swell! We'll take a midnight ride to town and back! But why? Everything is closed in town. Any special reason?"

No. Reason is knowledge. The intellect again. I had not the least knowledge why. But I had to obey "or else" begin to lose the intuition that grows stronger only by exercising itself in the muscles as well as the brain and imagination. One has to carry them out if anywhere within reason — these strange inner urges that I had determined to follow to the end.

So we went. And ahead of us on the road was a pile of leaves such as drift up like snow impelled by the late fall winds. I have driven through dozens of windrows of leaves like that. But this time I stopped the car with the headlights on the pile of leaves and asked my boys to kick through it. Beneath the leaves was a log big enough to have wrecked our car, had we not stopped. The boys carried it to the side of the road, and as we stood there trying to decide whether to go on to town or not, since my urge had vanished with the removal of the log, a car speeded through, going sixty mile an hour at least. It plowed through the leaves where the log had been, and the group of teenagers in it, on their way home from a show, yelled a greeting to us as they passed.

A useful if thankless job on our part. The life of half a dozen youngsters could hang on a "hunch" to drive to town and back, in the middle of the night. But to foresee the sinking of an unknown ship, and to sense the shock of public reaction, was of no help whatever to anyone.

But all such experiences are not fruitless. Often a connection came to light later that was wholly unknown to me at the time. A

95

striking example of this occurred later in connection with one of our worst storms on Lake Michigan.

While listening to the wind, I "imagined" and described to several witnesses the plight of a sailing vessel, a schooner, with masks broken, and sails torn to shreds. The crew abandoned hope and were expecting to go down with the hull when it sank.

In order to see if we could sight anything, six of us went over to the lakeshore. The wind and sand cut our faces, and we could hardly stay on our feet. We saw nothing.

One of our party, Jack, who knew ships, said he did not think there was any such schooner as I had described left in the Great Lakes trade. But even if it were true, what could we do about it? Why my apprehension, which persisted for hours, that took me out into the storm when I might have stayed where it was warm and dry?

Other ships were in danger; one of our own boats went over in White Lake, and my sons had been getting it in before joining us at Lake Michigan. A ship to the south of us sank. A hundred ships could go down in this storm, and I would not know it or feel any more than a general concern. It was this one imagined schooner, like a bird with broken wings that fretted me as if I ought to be able to do something about it. But what? There was not a boat within miles that could have survived an attempted rescue, even if I could have proved that the whole matter existed outside my imagination.

But not until Meredith asked me if I thought there was any hope for them did my mind leave the general direction of where I felt the schooner to be, and "scan" the rest of the lake.

Finally, I said, "There is a big freighter way to the north. It looks like a long black cigar. It is the only ship that could save them, but it is heading out of the storm in another direction. There is only one slim chance for that schooner. If the captain of the ship follows the hunch he ought to be feeling right now, he will change his course. Then he might sight them."

It seemed pretty hopeless, even granting it were all true. But we all threw our thoughts at the captain of an imaginary freighter like a long black cigar, hoping to strengthen the "hunch" that he ought to feel, if there were really a sailing vessel out there with only hours left to stay afloat.

But how many follow their hunches? What captain in his right mind would turn back into a storm at the command of a feeble little twitch somewhere in his brain or spine or solar plexus? With a wind so loud that his second officer would have to shout to be heard, could he be expected to hear the unspoken prayer of men facing death, or the thoughts of strangers standing on the shore more than a hundred miles away?

But there was a connection, and I did not know it. The captain of the freighter, that long black cigar, was not only a "reality," he was my old friend Captain Charles Mohr, to whom I had predicted that he would sail a ship before he ever laid hands on one, whom I taught to follow his hunches, predicting that if he did so he would be honored above all other Great Lakes captains, and go down in history and the annals of navigation on the Great Lakes. He had years before agreed with me to follow his hunches as an experiment, and let me know the results.

One of the results was not only one but five lake rescues, saving twenty-seven lives. But this was the climax of his career. For this he was to be honored as the first Great Lakes captain ever to receive the Congressional Medal. Here was the one man afloat on the lake in that storm who not only could experience a "hunch," but who, by agreement with me, made a practice of obeying it when he did.

Captain Mohr has passed on, but he still lives in the memory of all who knew him as a man who stood alone in the hour of his decision, upon which the lives of seven men depended. He stood alone, not only against the judgment of his men, but against the better judgment of his own intellect. He did respond to the thoughts and needs of other men, not only on one but on many occasions.

I remember the time when a young man told me how he stood, when a boy, on the Michigan Avenue Bridge in Buffalo, watching the then magnificent ship *Merida* come in, and wishing that someday he could be a captain of a fine ship like that. I told him that he could, that if he sincerely wished it, he was prophesying for himself, and that if he followed his intuition and always obeyed his "hunches," he not only could be the captain of a ship like that, but make a name for himself to be honored with the finest recognition ever to have been received by a Great Lakes navigator.

He became a captain, and his first ship was the *Merida*. I received a letter from him later:

The afternoon we had the talk together, you said that after I got home there would be a letter for me from Chicago from a heavy thick man by the name of J.—John, you thought— and through him I would get a good job sometime in March. But before that I would have two other offers which I would

97

take but wouldn't keep. Well, it all came to pass within a day or so from the time you had predicted, except that the man's name is Jeremiah, instead of John. You said I was to sail a big boat successfully, which I did, and that I was to have a little girl born. I've got that too.

Offer No. 2, as per your prediction. You said I would have an offer from the East in February, also that it would be from Buffalo. If you remember I said more likely from Cleveland. You said possibly so, but every time you mentioned it you said Buffalo, just as you said it would, and I have accepted it.

When Captain Mohr received the Congressional Medal and his five lake rescues were cited, he sent me a clipping, and wrote, "My reasons for sending this to you is because it is just what you told me would happen over fifteen years ago, and I have not forgotten."

This is but one instance among many in the experience of one man besides myself. He is but one of several thousand witnesses in the files of my own mental experiments. And there are thousands of others in the world today who have had similar experiences, and who, even at the moment that I write this, and again as you read it, know the truth of such things beyond any possible doubt.

In the face of all the evidence that is available in the world today, the opinion of men who doubt because they have had no such experience deserves the same consideration as the skepticism of the Kentucky mountaineer, who refused to believe that radio was true because he did not possess one.

The experience of others will not convince you like an experience of your own. It is not something you can learn from books. I have hoped to show you the way to find out for yourself, but a better understanding of your own experience is in comparing them with mine.

The intuitive life itself has no problems save those that vanish in solving themselves. For it is not really necessary to understand everything, so long as intuition succeeds in translating itself into successful action. Obedience to the promptings of intuition removes by prevention all problems that disobedience would create.

But he who sets out to live the life of intuition in collaboration with the intellect (a modern necessity) finds himself obliged to correlate and harmonize science, philosophy, and religion. He must harness intuition by "logic, reason, and common sense." And in so doing he encounters the critical demands of the intellect to provide adequate explanation and verbal representation. And he must squarely face and answer for himself by experience the questions: "Is man a mere electrical recording machine?" "Is he also a 'radio'?" And if the second, "What is the source of the broadcasting he receives?" Is it possible to 'talk without thinking'? (i.e. to by-pass the intellect), and if so, "What 'puts the words into one's mouth'?"

From childhood I had found it necessary to "stop thinking" in order to "imagine" correctly. But as I grew older, I found that if I stopped thinking while talking, words were actually "put into my mouth" and I would say things that were verified as correct without having the least idea what I was talking about, and without requiring any exercise of imagination or understanding on my part.

A similar phenomenon occurred in writing. I could take a blank piece of paper and write on it something I never knew or thought of before. But it was definitely not so-called automatic writing. I simply said or wrote what popped into my mind at the instant; and it popped out of my verbal memory instead of my memory of scenes and pictures (as in the case of "imagining" things), but I would not know what I was going to say or write next. And I was always astonished on reading it over afterward, or hearing the reaction of my listener, to discover that it not only "made sense," but was something that could be verified.

The trouble with most people is that they shape things to suit themselves, according to past acquirements, whereas we should permit truth to come to us, crystallizing in its own shape. We should then try to figure out what the shape is.

Some "feel" things without seeing any mental "pictures." Some have vague "hunches" that act only at forks in the road, to aid them in determining which direction to take at the moment, but without providing them with any clear vision concerning their goal or the means of attaining it.

Some visualize their ideals in all, then carry them out one by one, prophesying for themselves without realizing it. And some sense things only through symbols, which constitute a universal language of understanding based on memory element of sensory experience in nature. The intuitive dreams and "imaginings" of this type of person will seldom be literally true. The truth is embodied in symbols that must be interpreted.

The history of human experience is filled with cases of all kinds, but in my investigation of these things I have personally experienced all types of mental phenomena without finding it necessary to take the word of anyone else for anything. I have seen thousands of "false pictures" in my "mind's eye" of things that have actually happened, of things happening at the moment, and of future events. But often I see a symbol that I must interpret, and in talking with my friends of the symbols that come to me, it has often been the case that they knew exactly what I was talking about when it was still a mystery to me.

One day, for example, I was talking with a man in connection with whose initials I imagined that I saw the symbol of a silver frog. Two common conceptions of my memory, "silver" and "frog," were thus compounded by my intuition in an apparent but vain effort to communicate something to my intellect. I could not make sense out of it, nor could the man in question at the time of our conversation.

But later he informed me, "You know that silver frog you spoke of? Well, the two middle names that I never use, save for the initials, originally meant a silversmith and a tadpole."

Another case was my first conversation with a Mr. H. of Grand Rapids. I told him that when I shook hands with him, I saw mentally many houses in construction, but it puzzled me a great deal because there did not seem to be any evidence of their being occupied at any time.

This didn't make sense to me, but Mr. H. and his friend Mr. W. were very much amused, as one of the projects that Mr. H. was then interested in launching was a new kind of toy, a peculiar kind of building blocks with which children could easily construct substantial houses of several miniature sizes, depending on the number of blocks used.

Another source of confusion in many experiences of mental phenomena is the difficulty of discerning between "thoughts" of people and events that actually take place. The effect of the "mass mind" must always be guarded against by an intuitive person in his relation with public affairs.

In my own experience I found it necessary to attempt to shut out "thoughts" altogether on such occasions, in order to get at the "facts."

Is "impersonal vision" possible? When I was asked if I could "imagine" or describe something that was going on in the world elsewhere, and specifically when I was asked if I could describe the greatest crime being committed in the city of Chicago at the moment (and it turned out that I was correct), to what extent was telepathy involved? Did some human mind or minds have to be seeing or remembering? Was my imagination of the crime an "impersonal vision," or was it induced by the activity of the criminal's mind?

Does human memory survive death, and if so, is it possible for disembodied minds to witness earthly events and to induce a representation of them in the imagination of a living person? Can the imagination of a living person envision distant senses or inanimate objects without the aid of witnessing minds, living or dead?

Are conclusive answers to these questions possible on the basis of the experimental evidence available? I do not think so. One may believe what one will. Only this fact remains: the "vision" is there. Your "human radio" and "mental vision" are working. But you do not know with certainty who or what is broadcasting what you receive — and you do not know where it is coming from.

Consider the following experience to which well-known witnesses are still living and available, though two are dead. We were on "location" during the filming of one of a number of moving pictures in which I was interested. A number of us, including the director, the late James Cruze, were sitting on a bench in a park near Hollywood, while preparations were being made for the nest scene.

There was an old man, an extra hired for the day, tapping the ground idly with the point of his cane. He was out of hearing, and also deaf. On the spur of the moment, I said to the others on the same bench with us and in adjacent chairs, "Do you want to see me make that old man draw a triangle in the sand with his cane, and then make a figure in the center of it?"

Everyone on the bench and within hearing held his breath almost, under the impression that I was concentrating as an experiment in trying to influence the old man telepathically to do what I had said. I was thinking about it, of course, and watching the old man intently. But the thoughts in my mind, far from being an effort to "will" the old man to do as I said, were somewhat as follows: "Now what made me say that? I have put myself on a spot, and without any good reason for doing so."

For a moment or two the old man continued his tapping. Then suddenly taking a new grip on his cane, he began making aimless and disconnected dashes, lines instead of dots. In another moment he dragged the cane back and forth in zigzag line. He ended up by making a clearly defined triangle, and then proceeded to interest himself in drawing something inside it.

Everyone present thought it was a clearly defined case of telepathic influence or "thought transference," without the conscious

101

cooperation or knowledge of the subject. Of more interest to me were the reactions of the individuals who had witnessed the little performance. They ranged from excitement to amazed incredulity. But the entire episode ended in a burst of laughter, because of the tone of voice in which Jimmy Cruze uttered one of his characteristic and good-humored, but unprintable curses, when he saw what the old man had done.

He capped a vivid description of what he would be by the exclamation, "By God! You did it!"

I said, "Hold on now, Jimmy. Don't jump to any conclusions. I may have done it, but I'm not convinced of it."

This seemed to astonish him more than the little experiment. He said, "What are you talking about? I don't get it. Didn't I see it?"

"Think it over. Did I really make the old man carry out my whim of the moment, or did I merely predict what he was going to do?"

But the next scene was ready. Jimmy got up and lumbered away, mumbling "Merely!"

He was not in the least impressed by the distinction, but it was a real one. In thousands of similar cases the material evidence provides no direct proof whether the prediction or statement involves mental processes that cause the event, or whether the event, casting its shadow before it, causes the statement.

Chapter VIII

We can no longer hold, even from the scientific view, to the conceptual belief that the physical universe within the range of our five special senses comprises the whole of reality. We know that by far the greater portions of it are "unseen," and that our personal environing realities contain both cosmic and atomic elements with which our five recognized senses are unable to deal. Still, we do deal with them by means of speech and conceptual thought. And conspicuous among the words and concepts that serve us for this purpose are "God" and the "atom," the one manifesting in religious behavior and the other in scientific behavior.

No one has seen God, and no one has seen a single atom. So far as these or any other concepts manifest in human behavior (serving as guides to action or research), it makes not the slightest difference whether they are "true" or not. But the knowledge of God has come to man in the same way as any of the generalizations of science.

We define "magnetism" as that unknown cause or power to which the magnetic force of our experience is due. We may define" gravity" as that unknown cause or power to which the gravitational forces of our experience are due. And we may define "God" as that unknown cause or power to which are due those compulsions of human experience that are to be found in love, faith, inspiration, and so on, and which transcend sex, our ability to reason, and our capacity as rational animals to understand.

Thus, as far as man transcends sex and self in his relation with others, he has admitted into his life of emotion and behavior something "above" nature, i.e., something "supernatural." For nature contains sex and life, but not love and inspiration, by which alone the beast in man is subdued to permit a higher evolutionary process.

Today, we are all the victims of world conditions that have been brought about by power politics without love, as devised by intellect without God. We have been smothered mentally by a great logomachy (war of words without deeds) as an intellectual smoke screen of propaganda to hide what is really going on. For we have been living in a primitive state of world civilization dominated by purely rational animals in the form of self-preservative men, among whom the process of reasoning has reigned supreme as intellect without God. And the future outlook of such a civilization (in which material progress has exceeded spiritual development) is dismal indeed *unless we can learn to understand and preserve a world-wide peace in an age of atomic weapons.*

Science is now fully aware of this conditional outlook. But religion has for ages had priority over the best methods of controlling human behavior. And only now, when forced by circumstances to do so, scientists are waking up to the fact that the only alternative to the way of religion, i.e., love and faith, is the way of totalitarian regimentation by fear, discipline and force. For it has been found (too late to prevent damage already done) that knowledge and intelligence are not enough to create and maintain righteousness in the world. Neither scientific nor philosophic or liberal literary education is capable of preserving peace on earth through human behavior.

The situation is ironic. For many of our most intelligent men hve in the past half century turned from religion because they were unable to accept the various faiths, dogmas, and doctrines as "true." They have reared and educated a generation of young rationalists, some of whom are still open-minded as agnostics, and some of whom are aggressive and even militant theists. And now (again too late to undo the damage) we find scientific rationalists realizing that the "truth" of a faith (as they define the truth) is entirely irrelevant to the survival value and progress value of its function in human behavior.

What people believe manifests in their behavior *whether or not it be "true" by any criterion whatever.* And here is where scientific men have made the greatest and most costly error of all history: in assuming that the scientific criterion of truth could be applied to the evaluation of human speech and conceptual thought as manifest in beliefs and opinions.

It is not necessary for human ideas to correspond with past or present realities *in order to create future realities through human behavior.* The test of faith is not in "facts" but in "works." The sole virtue and only legitimate psychological criterion of truth (as applied to human belief) is prophetic. The power and truth of a word or a conceptual thought is creative. It acquires meaning or truth only when it is "made flesh" in deeds, action, behavior.

From this view the scriptures of the world take on astonishing significance. Doubt if you will, but, unless you believe, nothing happens to change the biological behavior pattern of yesterday. For since man can think only with what he already possesses to think with, he resists change until experience makes it a part of his memory. Hence religion in its purely intellectual or speculative aspects has

104

derived largely from the fact that man doubts, hence gives birth to reason in order to believe what he fears to doubt.

These rationalized beliefs may or may not be "true," and so far as they are effective in the constructive guidance of human behavior, it does not matter. The true secret of life can be known only by him who is able to eliminate the mental concept of life. Neither sense impressions, words, nor mental concepts are capable of encompassing the truth of whole situations. But they provide data whereby intuition with the aid of memory and imagination integrates and synthesizes this sensory data together with extra-sensory assistance into a more complete understanding than a merely logical method of reasoning can provide.

This leads to the realization that truth is not to be defined in terms of the evolving organism and its sensations, or reactions to sensations, but in terms of the environing reality to which ultimate adaptation is essential both for self-realization and for the continued progress of survival.

Only intuition escapes words and concepts, including space and time. Only intuition can evoke from memory in imagination those recombinations that make up new and prophetic concepts to meet the needs of further progress. The only alternative to our self-guidance on the path of evolutionary progress by the costly trial-and-error, hit-or-miss method of rational experimentation is in the dynamic inspiration of a psychological orthogenesis evoked by intuitive faith.

It has been said that "man is created in the likeness or image of God." Science is unable either to affirm or to deny such a statement. But a scientific investigation of God (I speak as one who has for fifty years been engaged in such an investigation) does lead directly to the proposition that God manifests in the likeness of man (for man) and in the likeness of nature (for nature). If one dips water from the ocean, the water will take the shape of one's cup. And we must investigate and analyze the water as we find it in that cup. Thus a personal God is the basis of individual and sociological evidence of a phenomenal nature. So we say, on the basis of such evidence, that "God is Love." And we affirm this God of man as his Creator, not in a historic, but in a dynamic, and immediate, and a prophetic sense. For creation is continuous—*and man is not Man as yet.*

It is precisely because man is free to accept or reject the "Substance of things hoped for, the [intuitive] evidence of things unseen" that a scientific investigation of human faith is possible. We can learn more about the kind of love that is Godlike than we can about gravity, for the very reason that life is possible without love, whereas it is impossible to escape gravity for the sake of comparison.

The historians, the psychologists, the sociologists, and the editorial commentators have long been at work analyzing the origins of present-day, world-wide conflict. We have heard all about the war-mongering of profiteers, power politics, population pressure, ideological differences, and so on. But all these things are consequences—not one of them goes deeply enough to get at the source of the trouble. It has taken centuries for man to recognize in the "new commandment" of Jesus, not a mystical, but a scientific prescription for the world's ills.

Still, some of us knew. Years ago, a scientific friend half-jokingly asked, "Can you tell me in two words what it is all about—what is really the cause of all this turmoil and confusion in the world today?" He did not really mean "two words." That was just a figure of speech to him, but I accepted the challenge. I replied, "Sexual accidents." And by this I meant "unwanted children" who, unloved and the fruit of loveless unions, grew up to manifest not only the "population pressure," but the neurotic behavior, the compensatory substitution of selfish motives, excessive intellectual specializations, and the internal conflicts that are evident in the external conflicts of the world today. The world's wanted children are being sacrificed to universal sexual and intellectual perversion. From loveless soil spring the personnel of war-mongering and the power politics of intellect without God.

But "intellect without 'God" does breed its own destruction. There are signs that the splitting of the atom has brought the Age of Reason to an end. Reluctantly, the somewhat dazed intellectual individualists are being forced to admit that they belong to a biological brotherhood from which they are unable to withdraw, that there are "many members but one Body," and that the harmony of its parts depends upon behavior that neither science nor philosophy have thus far been able to induce.

Now we find thousands displaying a credulity and hunger for any assurance bearing the semblance of truth, and with a thirst for faith miracles, and a humility of childlike appeal as if proud "reason" had never claimed and wielded world-wide supremacy.

And it now appears that the works of the intellect have advanced man not an inch from the view of ultimate survival value. We find even scientists once more admitting that they have arrived at the solution of many problems in a manner "indistinguishable from

106

inspiration." We see articles in the press and in journals and in books revealing that "Science has discovered Love and is prescribing it as medicine," "Power of suggestion and faith result in cures that puzzle medical science," "Doubts plague scientists; skeptical of 'knowledge,' they turn to mathematical yardstick," "Religion needed to meet atomic power challenge," and so on.

But did we not know this all the time? Were not the Golden Rule, the doctrine of love, the works of intuitive faith, the poverty of knowledge without God, and the correlativity of Christ all simply set forth in the words of Jesus? Was not this enough? Evidently it was not, for men failed to understand it as a profound gospel of far-seeing and prophetic scientific value. And in order to become effective universally, it has had to be established as such, and it has had to be freed from its basis of belief based on authority, by wide phenomenal reaffirmations.

To understand all this, and to avoid the errors of misinterpretation that perpetuates the vicious circles of religious-scientific logomachy, we must escape the tyranny of words that keeps the pendulum of reactionary minds ever swinging between skepticism and mysticism. Billions of words have poured from the presses of periodicals and publishers — to the confusion of those who seek for truth and understanding outside themselves. Men have ever rushed here and there, crying, "Truth! Truth!" where it does not matter — and rejecting it where it does.

Let them consider the answer that was given to the young Egyptian medical student (in *King of Dreams*) when he asked his wise old teacher whether he believed that the Master of Healing was truly Son to the Lord of Life and had walked on earth, or was it a fable?

The teacher asked, "Do you think that it matters?"

Said the student, "I think it does matter whether we are taught the truth or lies."

"Then tell me, what is truth?" asked the teacher.

"Why — " but the student could not answer.

Said the teacher, "Yes, it is like that. We draw Truth with her feather, and call her co-worker with the Lord of Life, but we do not know her, nor can we hold her. We say, 'There is truth in that man's heart.' But did you search that heart with your scalpel, you would but thrust her forth to seek another home — you would not find her.

???

Truth is not a thing of flesh and blood, but of the spirit. That is why I say it does not matter whether or not our Master was divine and walked on earth, for his spirit is among us now wherever there is charity and the desire to heal. Men make their gods — I do not say they make them out of nothing, or that no great Ones ever came down from Heaven in pity for our need — and while men are, they will comfort their souls with the image of some Good Physician who cares for them, though they may not always call him Imhotep of Memphis. Again, in ages to come men of your blood and mine in Alexandria may forget Isis, whom we call Our Lady. But because so long as men love their mothers they will worship motherhood, our far-off descendants will bow before the images of another Mother and another Child. Nor will one faith be truer than the other, for Truth is eternal and faiths are but her perishable garments."

     ???

Wise were the teachers of old who taught man never to speak the "Everlasting Name." For to speak it is but to record it on the graphophone records of human intellects, and there to rob it of power and meaning by endless repetition of mechanical utterance. And thus man substitutes a false god in a mental concept that intelligent men are perfectly right to "deny." For it is nothing but a mental echo and a vibration of the human larynx to which men bow in their ignorance, while the very soul of man, the spark of god within him, cries out against it, saying, "That is not I!"

Chapter IX

Not everything is easy to explain, but we must avoid attaching the "mystery" to the wrong gate. The prime mystery is no longer in the physiological and nervous organization of man—no more than in the construction of the Geiger counter. The mystery is in the so-called cosmic rays that act on the Geiger counter. What are they, and where are they from?

The mystery is in the source of energy, or life, that acts on or in the nervous organization of man to produce an intuitive "feeling." What is it, and where is it from? There need be no other mystery. The organism upon which it acts is now fairly well known. New ductless glands will be discovered. Many neural functions and operations will be better understood. But in all the essentials the physiological foundation and nervous organization of man is well enough understood in the light of developments in the field of electronics and radiant energy, to know that man is capable of experiencing *feelings* independent of seeing, hearing, smelling, tasting, touching—feelings that result from responses to stimuli emanating from sources known or unknown.

Beyond this coordinated sensitivity of the entire nervous system, no further or special sense is required. It is superfluous to postulate mysterious powers of vision, clairvoyance, clairaudience, psychic ability, and so on, when the normal powers and *modus operandi* of imagination and memory not only suffice in explanation, but may be investigated experimentally to establish the fact that one's so-called psychic faculties or extrasensory perceptions are entirely limited, constituently, to the contents of the individual memory, just as the constituents of words are limited to the alphabet employed, and one's verbal representation is limited to one's vocabulary unless one pauses to look up or coin a word for an idea that has not yet been incorporated by identification in one's verbal memory.

And yet I have personally had words come to mind and pass over my tongue in experimental conditions, words entirely unfamiliar to me, words in foreign language, or technical terms that could be found in a dictionary (though previously unfamiliar to me), and some that could not—words conveying information that I did not myself know, but which was afterward verified as correct. Still, I used familiar syllables. I used the familiar alphabet.

And even when I inscribed hieroglyphics entirely unfamiliar to me, it was a composition of familiar smaller elements of lines and

109

curves, shapes, and angles. The fact still remains that my vision of these things cannot correctly be described in terms so vastly misleading and misunderstood as "psychic," "telepathic," and so on. It was nothing whatever but imagination compositing familiar elements of previous sensory experience recorded in memory.

I see and correctly describe a scene ten thousand miles away. (I have done this under experimental conditions with witnesses.) I see and describe a future event that occurs exactly as I have described it, save for minor variations. What is lacking or faulty in my description is lacking in my memory. For what do I see? Nothing but my own imagination. Actually, I do not see ten thousand miles away with any form of "vision" whatever. I do not "see" the future. My reception or perception of these things is entirely formless, entirely a "feeling," entirely devoid of images, words, thought, or concept. What makes it intelligible to me or someone else is the activity of my imagination, which endeavors to symbolize, to portray, to interpret the "feeling."

The reality is the energy that cannot be destroyed. What we know as "life" is but an echo and shadow, the organic reflex of the radiant energy that sustains the Great Broadcasting Program of Nature. If we attempt to attune ourselves more completely in accord with the Great Central Broadcasting Station of this mammoth program of life, the act of so doing is called "prayer." The vibration that chills our spine when we make the attunement--why should we not regard it as a "holy spirit" and the source of the energy, the "something else"? What does it matter what we call it?

The prophets of every nation and of every epoch have risen to proclaim the conception of a living God. Modern science has approached the threshold and is trying to explain this living God by drinking, tasting, hearing, seeing, smelling, and feeling under the name of energy; and the "holy spirit" of this God of Science is radiant energy.

Unless this all-pervading living God of immediate inspiration is infused into the churches, temples, synagogues, and shrines, to replace the intellectual God of yesterday (a God in word, concept, and memory only), the power to resuscitate the people will fade, even as an echo after the voice and ceased to vibrate, and individuals will in ever-increasing number seek God outside the church. And there they will find Him either in silence and alone, by joining some small, private group, or by falling prey to the cults and -isms that live like parasites on human credulity and sincerity.

For man seeks the "gate to power." He wants the success, love, life, happiness, and realization that power brings. And if the key to spiritual power is withheld from him, he substitutes material power — and starves in the midst of his wealth.

It is not enough that the power of prophecy existed twenty centuries ago. It is not enough to hear sermons about it. He wants, and he has a right to, the fulfillment of those promises: "Even ye can do greater things than I," and "Each shall prophesy that all may be comforted." This cannot be hidden from him by shelving the records of scripture or retranslating them to leave out the word "prophesy," both of which have upon occasion been done.

The seed of all this is in man's intuition to sprout anew, and he is not to be robbed of his birthright by conspiracies of the intellect that have ever enslaved the souls of men. The moisture and warmth to release this power is found in tears of sorrow and compassion, and in faith, of which one's prayer is but the barometer. When we do not pray, we have lost faith in our soul, our "radio" is silenced, and only our memory of self speaks to us — but in empty words and self-pity, which encourages our vanity to silence conscience.

It is only the intellect that doubts, and that can maintain a state of activity entirely devoid of relation to truth. But the one and essential power that distinguishes the complicated nervous organization of man from the simpler one of the animal is the power of recombination, by means of which the imagination can make new creations out of the memory element of old experience.

Thus we symbolize, we indulge in fantasy, we speculate and theorize, we create works of art, we invent, and thus we produce a culture and a civilization. But as we thus change environments, we change our "destiny," and we change the character of adaptation that operates in the law of the survival of the fit. Just as instinct no longer suffices as a mechanism of adaptation in intellectual environments, so does intellect fail to suffice as a mechanism of adaptation in the world of human progress and competition, which has been fathered by "flashes of genius" that have harnessed the power of nature without harnessing the power of human nature to make the right use of them.

Neither instinct nor intellect can cope with life in such a world. Inspiration and intuition become necessities. Without the guidance of spiritual values, mere knowledge betrays us. Without religion (not doctrinal religion, but a religion of inspiration to provide intuitive guidance as a substitute for the instinct, which intellect has forfeited), science can but lead us to destruction.

111

It becomes increasingly necessary to "imagine" correctly, to adapt oneself to more subtle and more complicated environments, to develop foresight as well as a knowledge of consequences; to plan, to prepare, to prevent. We find that only those who do this survive. Intuition becomes a necessity. And the very life of intuition is prayer.

In its broad sense prayer is an expression of religious need or mood, any form of religious self-expression by means of which attunement with the cosmos is sought or attained. But in man this is wholly intuitive, just as an animal's biological adaptation to the environing realities of nature is instinctive and instinct-forming. With these processes of biological adaptation, the human intellect may, and to some extent does, collaborate; but to a larger extent it has set itself in defiance against them. Witness the world turmoil of the present century, as well as past ages of mental confusion, to behold the works of "intellect without God" in a world in which effectual prayer is a "lost art."

Religion is expressed in worship. The origin of worship is assumed to have been in primitive efforts to perform acts that were thought to be pleasing to the Deity. In so doing, the worshiper experienced emotional consequences that he interpreted as evidence of divine favor. Thus the intellect gave birth to an art as a form of exercise, public or private, that was performed as a matter of divine prescription, or as an expressing of one's feelings of relationship to Deity.

The first grew into ritual, i.e., the repetition of regular and traditional practices the validity of which becomes entirely irrelevant so long as they result in the psychological consequences they were designed to produce. But the second remained spontaneous, the free and extemporaneous expression of feeling, a witness to the immediacy of religious experience and its individual character. This aspect of worship is the very substance of the intuitive life, and the highest form of prayer.

When people complain that their prayers are not answered, then either they have not fulfilled the necessary conditions or they know neither how to pray nor what prayer is. "Ye ask, and receive not, because ye ask amiss."

Those who pray that the flame that envelops their entire house may be extinguished at once have been unbalanced by the shock of being caught unprepared. Prayer will not controvert common sense. Even God cannot help here, for god's law was obeyed when the house caught fire. Why was it not prevented by the one in charge? Why resort to prayer at the last moment in any matter that might have been prevented but that was previously ignored?

Prayer is a reminder to "tune in," so that you will take care of the matches and gasoline before they become instruments of a big blaze. Prayer is a comforter. It is a hope restorer. But if a man thinks that God is going to listen to him when he pleads on his knees in prayer to save his life at eighty, after having forgotten Him for seventy-nine years, he is entirely ignorant of the nature and function and purpose of prayer. But if one has been sincere and fair in all his dealings, he has been praying all the time, and his prayers are answered before he knows it. And he is pleased. And so is God.

If we are guided by the correction principles, if we live by the "golden rule" and refrain from coveting what belongs to others, then our sincere heart's desires are the foreshadowing of their own fulfillment, just as a seed foreshadows the fruit. Our effort to discern and to submit them for spiritual sanction ("Not my will, but thine") is but a mode of divination. Our prayer born of faith is the prophecy made manifest—the answer, not the petition (which was already manifest in our natural and wholly reasonable and God-implanted aspirations and ideals).

It is only the intellect that is capable of ineffectual prayer. To offset this, Jesus of Nazareth (He who demonstrated the power of effectual prayer in a life of action) invented a verbal safeguard. He taught His followers what was known as the Lord's Prayer, to guide man in his blindness through self-created dark hours or ages, his anchor or hope held firm on rocks of abstract truth, until the light of inspiration once again breaks through the mental clouds of worldly chaos, to restore his heritage of the lost art of intuitive living, which is rewarded by the faith that sanctifies and guarantees the power and the effectiveness of his prayer.

The prayer that opens the gates of the mind through man's mental "radio" and "television" is a mental-emotional attitude, not a ritual of words. It is a speechless outflinging of unseen antennae of nerves, by which man attunes himself to the "something else," the "universal element," the very source of his own being, across the gulf that only prayer can bridge by human radio.

And a "human radio" can do or ask no more than this. We climb the highest mountain of human endeavor, only to find, as others found before us, that within ourselves we are nothing. The soul within us, if not sleeping, is but the interception by our nervous system of the great Broadcasting Program of Man.

113

So when at last in my search for truth I had found my home, and made for myself a shrine of solitude where I could live an intuitive life and hear this program without distraction, I learned that labor was the wise man's prayer.

I began to pray the prayer of perspiration, tilling the field and kneeling at the altar of nature to plant my seeds, chopping wood to sacrifice upon the altar of fire for the purification, the shaping, and the tempering of the iron and steel that symbolized our flesh and blood.

For a pulpit I made a workbench where I preached sermons in science without words, but by the work of my hands; where the smell of fresh-cut sawdust was my incense, and my prayers as those of the builders who sought to obey the law of the plumb, the level, and the square.

Is this idolatry? No. For it has a meaning. It is idolatry only when one worships or attunes oneself to the body and not the soul, to the symbol when ignorant of its meaning, to the idol instead of the Deity it represents, to the dollar instead of the bread of life it can buy, to the echo instead of the voice, to the mental concept instead of the living power to do. It is idolatry to worship by words without works, to socialize rituals exacting obedience to the letter, when ignorant of the spirit of truth.

And this is the truth that I learned in the desert, and proved to myself through the passing years: *the flesh cannot pray.* A sincere prayer is but an echo of God's voice. God manifests Himself in our thoughts. He but whispers, and it becomes an echo in our prayers. Long before we ask for anything we have a right to ask, it is known and answered by an order that constitutes our faith. Thus faith is the sanction that our prayers are prophetic. And thus we reach the fulfillment of the intuitive life.

Then we learn anew that human brotherhood is possible only between intuitive men. Between wholly intellectual men only superficial and contractual bonds are possible. In marriage or in friendship "whom God hath bound, no man can put asunder." But only the intuitive bonds are thus binding in life or in death. For of such is the love that is God.

"How knoweth this man letters, never having learned?"

He is a Son of solitude. Throughout the ages and throughout the world, he constitutes that brotherhood of man that is sensitive by inspiration to the mutual welfare that is "God's will," and that therefore gives body to a great kingdom of silence to that invisible theocracy, which, in spite of selfish usurpers, has ever controlled the hidden springs of human progress, writing in deeds the history of the world.

Man can go where he will on board the ship of this world, but in going with the ship he can go no faster or slower, for running madly back and forth on the decks. If one man fails to obey the commands of the captain of that ship, another will endeavor to do so—perhaps in a different way, but to the same end. Did you not hear the human radio broadcast at three o'clock this morning? Well, I did—so that message will be delivered in my words if not in yours.

If the boiler does not burst out in one place, it will in another. History, like water, finds its level, regardless of the paths chosen or accepted by resignation to gravity on the part of individual drops.

The "play" has been written; the cast of characters has been "fixed." But the players of those parts remain to be selected for each performance.

In each generation "many are called but few are chosen." All aspirants must qualify, but the aspiration is the very voice of the necessary qualifications.

Men fail to realize that their very existence is the function of a "pressure," a power to which their "will" is not the steed but the harness, not the water, but the pipe and faucet.

The amount of pressure or power available is beyond the individual will or harness or pipe to determine. One may be left impotent or enabled to function with almost miraculous strength and understanding, according to whether or not he is playing his part as required by the Whole.

For thus wrote the hand of God in history—through the ambition, the energy, the enthusiasm, the inspiration, and the guidance that is provided for those who, wittingly or unwittingly, serve as instruments for the good of all, by power of intuition and love that is beyond individual comprehension.

The unwitting play their parts as puppets, and receive a puppet's wage. But he who knowingly seeks to serve mankind unselfishly is raised into the understanding of the great Exemplar of this age: He who first played the leading part that each of us may emulate, but that none can excel.

For the voice of intuition whispers: "He who travels through the desert of ignorance and the wild jungles of man's intellectual deformities in My name will be welcome in the green pastures of peace, wisdom, and love, where I dwell. So come unto me."

115

So the curtain rises on the next act in the spiritual drama of this world. The breeze is blowing over the prairie… *And the end is not yet.*

A Little Book of Crumbs from a Table Spread

Then the master of the house said to his servant, "Go out quickly into the streets and alleys of the city, and bring the poor, the maimed, the halt and the blind." The servant returned and said, "Lord, it is done as you have commanded, and still there is room."

— Luke 14:21-22

And these things matter most. It's not the amount of work we do, but the wages received for it. It's not our wages, but what we did to earn them. It's not our intentions, but our accomplishments. It's not what we liberate through our tongue, but what our eyes and ears record. It is not by force of will to conquer, but by receptivity to fact. It is not how we have lived, but how we are able to die. It's not what we have been, but what we are. It's not what we give, but how it is received. It's not that we give, but as we give. It's not what we teach, but what we practice. It is not the flower of genius that we carry while we live, but the century-plant of our efforts which blooms years after our dissolution. Yes, these things matter most. Mind is as little able to be mind without the consciousness of God, as without the consciousness of self.

Remember, there are no miracles, unless a leap from one point to another—and the gap that we have leaped is a law of Nature which we have omitted.

Often we absorb knowledge or food not meant for us, and of which, like a stain, we must rid ourselves in order to start anew.

Show me a man who has not made mistakes, and I will how you one who will soon make them.

Joy and pleasure is the law of gravitation that evolves unto spiritual perfection: if not amalgamated with sensuality and the animal propensities.

A fault once denied is twice committed.

In swatting a fly, you know, we often hit ourselves with more vigor than we intended.

Thoughts are wreathes of evaporating intelligence.

No matter how strong we may think we are, a few grains of sand thrown in the eyes will make us helpless.

He who thinks himself great, is that much more a coward; and to the extent of his greatness does he fear Death.

God places in our make-up future realities which can often be interpreted by our imagination or visualized pictures.

The past is the memory of the body or mind. The future is the memory of the soul.

Never measure what you are going to do by seconds, nor what you have done by minutes, but what you will do by centuries.

It often pays a man to protect his individuality by burning all bridges behind him.

Death is more natural than birth: Birth can be prevented, but Death never.

Do not allow anything to appear out of your reach. The fact that you can anticipate the possibilities, is evidence that you are entitled to them, and can realize them. A beginning appears hard because the end seems so far off—but who wants the end?

The greatest virtue of achievement is appreciation.

Be careful not to allow the weather-vane to stick, or it will lie.

Admiration is an unconsciousness confession of dormant accomplishments in the admirer.

When a masterpiece is in the making one must expect broken tools, dirt, and labor. But later comes the polishing, where only the dust remains to be swept away.

We often try short-cuts in life, trying to run a wide gauge car on a narrow gauge rail, and wonder why there are so many bumps. King or fool, act—live the part.

If you wish to become a butterfly, become a worm: for it is as essential to understand the stratas of God's footstool, with its darkest hour, as the air-currents in the brightest sunshine of joy.

A loyal friend despises secrets. A pretended one welcomes them.

The man who can blind himself to sorrow and pain, has all the joy of the Universe, and knows not the darkness in his blindness.

The really dangerous person is one who is impulsive in action. He explodes his imaginary grievances into action without reflection; while one who hesitates, and gloats in the thought of revenge, unconsciously uses a lightning rod and becomes harmless.

Let the man among us who is most efficient and capable lead the way, and let the rest of us thank God that we can serve.

The man who is sincere seldom advertises his intentions.

Our infirmities are only as we form them mentally, and allow them to escape unconsciously. Later they return with a large family. Loose impulses cause genius to turn to insanity, and the victim to lose the power of his compass.

Clothe an absolute necessity in beauty and charm, and not only will it be fashionable, but it will give birth to a greater beauty and loveliness: for a necessity is the shell of protection, God's gift, a chrysalis: a butterfly from a worm; from a man to a God.

When calamity comes, dilute it with past joys.

When a man complains to you, ask him what he demands, what he receives, and what he is worth. Nothing more need be said.

A great man will not trample on a worm; nor will he sneak to a king. The man who labors in silence and darkness possesses more power than the one who holds his hand above his head in broad daylight and proclaims his intentions.

What you have had will never buy you a good meal.

Do not get into the habit of believing, and making others believe that you have reached the height of your ambition. Remember that it is only the foundation whereupon your future edifice shall stand.

Everything has its price — which is a necessity. Beyond that it is luxury; beyond that, a curse.

Immortality always seeks the shade of Respectability.

Love has hope where reason dies of starvation.

One with beauty and charm is a child of luxury — the coat of the leopard. But the one who is the leopard's hide when shorn of its fur, but with the tough leather as protection, is a child of necessity to support the child of luxury.

Fortunate is the man who carries all the prismatic colors of life, so that he may adapt himself, or apply his judgments.

Thoughts are composed of what one's vitality consists of.

The ladder of a social climber leans against a cloud that has no silver lining.

The man who is insane has stepped on one end of his teeter-totter and stayed there.

The stolen toy is the symbol of the hangman's noose.

If you wish to be happy and successful, adopt a girl and a boy: Apprehension and Comprehension.

If a student does not make himself a part of everything, he is not a part of the Whole.

He that seeketh hath a house to build to live therein. But he that seeketh not, has not been born.

We can measure the value of a thing by the time it required to complete it.

The man that counts, is the one who will swallow things, say nothing, and await his chance. An empty barrel makes the most noise, and thunder, with all its racket, is harmless, because the silent flash of lightning has already destroyed. Let it thunder.

Realization of your wants brings death closer.

121

A fly woke me, irritated me — I killed it. It sought food. It forced me to end its life by its desire for food, and my irritation. Desire but hastens consummation, with irritation the medium. A nation desires greater territory. An irritation brings war!

I saw a picture of the masses on a treadmill — grinding, grinding, grinding. Grinding what? Only their bearings, for the want of unselfish oil.

Labor, discipline and self-control still the fire of impulsiveness, so the hand of virtue may lead on to fill the void created by environments contrary to the growth of enlightenment.

Education is the musical instrument upon which the Spirit of God plays music of truths.

The more noise one can endure, the less sensitive his intellectual ability. His mental faculties are tuned to coarse slow vibrations. His endurance is a scale of acquirements.

He who is convinced against his will, will soon forget.

An uncontrollable imagination indicates that there is no wall between the spiritual and the material.

The crucial test comes when you wash your hands: then if no stain remains, your conscience may be clear.

He who is penitent of sin is half forgiven; but he who confesses his sin in penitence is entirely forgiven because a penitent possesses a truthful conscience which bears witness and passes sentence, but one who also confesses sin, destroys his alter of false pride, and expiates his penance to become a pure child of righteousness.

A genius is but an opening through the Wall that upholds truth and wisdom.

When a man condemns you, tell him to buy a new set of rules and implements, and you won't have to tell him he lies.

Man will doubt immortality as long as his objective memory is a part of his judgment.

Ignorant faith is Instinct.

The person worthwhile is the one who can accomplish things out of his sphere, not flying just because he has wings.

The man who lives within the chamber of licentious thoughts, must expect to pay its rent.

Courage makes a good man better, a bad man worse, because it is the powder behind the bullet.

Why be burdened with tools if no use is made of them? If no timber, then lay them aside for a time and gather timber.

An envious man is made gloomy not only by his own cloud, but by another's sunshine.

A poor man should acquire the dignity of a rich man, and a rich man should live the life of a poor man.

Any environment feeding upon itself, brings deterioration and annihilation thru fermentation.

It is impossible to see one's own reflection in those who do not possess its likeness. No one is perfect. But the man who excels, flies his own colors.

Consider the hypocrite who constantly raises the flag of truce in times of peace, and cries aloud, "I am an honest, virtuous man." I would like to know who taught such a man that there ever existed dishonesty or vice, if he has not already dipped his hand in slime and suspicion. Or who told him he was naked when there were no clothes? And why try to blot out a sin that has not been committed? But thus the world is. Where there is flexibility of motion there is life.

The more one binds himself to society, the more of a slave he becomes to slaves.

A curse, name or criticism has only the value that the victim places upon it.

Many minds are pregnant. Few give birth. Still fewer live to mature.

I believe in laboring hard to offset the mental, so that I may stand on the see-saw of life, just above the fulcrum, the spot where good judgment and common sense are born.

From Birth we journey to Death: Death is our reward to Life.

Do not rush anything. Simply let each little cell burst as a bubble, deposit its sentiment, and, like the minutest bit of life in the coral, form a structure that is indestructible in all its beauty.

He receives the most reward who is expecting none.

The man that conquers himself, conquers his enemies.

He is safer to think what we intend to say, than to say what we intend to think.

One can often win by silence, where aggressiveness loses the battle.

What you create, that you are.

One may obtain mental clothing in blood stained Europe, but the clean, virgin soil of the West is the best place on earth either to interpret past history or solve future mysteries. If one will learn what the appetites of the human mind consist of, then he can feed food that will continuously call for more. And as the Baker is as glad to get rid of the bread as the hungry man is to eat and pay for it, there is no denying that knowledge was created to be applied and passed on, the circulating coin of the mind. For if we hold it, it becomes musty, and fanaticism is born. But if we pass it on, our ears hear more keenly, our eyes discern more clearly, and the tongue is more clever at repartee. It is only the clever man who can make a mistake and in the same breath use it as a comedy to cover the defect.

If you let Pride build a wall about you, Habit will build a trench.

Always bear in mind that the bravest and strongest warrior becomes helpless at the point of his own sword.

The spirit of serving is becoming to the high as well as the lowly, but dignity belongs to him who is able to uphold it.

We but grasp at the thing we would be, and fall back on the lap of false destiny.

In the name of Love and Charity give your surplus profits at your youth, so that they may be returned to you in old age as necessities.

If a piano is not tuned, you cannot play correctly. This does not prove that the player is wrong. The fault is with the instrument. God is good, but we are poor instruments, out of tune. When our thoughts embody divine

Ideals, we throw off the shackles of death.

Ask, and ye shall receive that which must be paid for. Ask not your desires, and the fulfillment shall be your wages.

Success: To create your own wants to meet unavoidable circumstances that will form a bond of love and happiness.

Enthusiasm is an outburst of a new discovery realized.

Just get into the game of being boys and girls. It is the most wonderful game in the world. Even the Master played it when He said "Suffer little children to come unto me. Forbid them not." As little children we can enter the Kingdom of Heaven — but not as old men and women: for they are left behind to clean the cobwebs of old Mother Earth.

As we think and act, so are we. Our thoughts leave an indelible mark upon our features, while our actions leave monuments in the graveyards of the memories of others.

He who used Truth as a weapon, makes many enemies, but creates one Friend.

Money cannot always cover sin, for though the barrel and hoops may be made of the strongest wood and iron, the acid of immortality may burn its way through, rot the wood, and rust the iron.

You go upon the mountain top, calling a name you do not mean, expecting the echo to repeat the name you do—and are despondent when you hear the result.

If through my charity I give thee a coin, and it fails to give birth to another by its Gift, then thou art not worthy to have received it, and it will but make thee lose another, having lost its seed. We need go to no one for proof of life and death. We can see and realize, so that, to us, it will be absolute knowledge, without assumption, without theory, without mysticism—simply the truth. And as for modern Christianity, ninety-nine percent of the workers do not believe entirely in their views which they can only assume to be true. The one percent feel the spirit of the Master, and are sincere thru the spirit of faith. If we should place all creeds and sects in a wine-press, we would obtain one drop of pure water, transparent, crystal-clear, the living diamond of truth, which is the one perfection, the creation and why we are.

When a man has something new, or claims a power above the ordinary, such as Prophecy, the masses flock to him and say, "Let us see. Let us see." The wiser people say, "I will wait until he has been established for five years. If he lasts that long he must have something, and then I will go to see him." The still wiser men say, "We will wait ten years." The students of philosophy say, "We will wait twenty years, or perhaps thirty years; and then, if he is still alive, we can be certain that he has something worth investigating." But the Philosopher says, "I will wait until the day of his death, and go to see him at the side of his death-bed to receive his message."

Bread for the Day

A Second Book of Crumbs
from a Table Spread

Bread for the Day

The mind must be fed.
But let us lay aside fine words and spiced dishes.
Let us set the wine aside until evening.
Let us sip the milk of our childhood — and live on Bread for a day...
You ask, "What is Truth?" Truth is an established principle,
A law unerring, fixed by the Creator of reality.
It can be acquired by man, sustained by reason and logic.
It is the criterion of God.
It is the existence within existence, or the soul of life.

One can dip from the water of Eternity, freeze it to the shape of a Christ — but neglect the thought materialized, and it will melt back to oblivion, to remain there until shaped again, according to the conception of the next seeker.

Man's understanding is limited. Beyond this limit he fails to grasp Truth. It is like going into a forest. One can go no further than the center without beginning to come out again.

While we possess this human conveyance we are taxed by its laws to obey its own mandates: a law onto itself which may conflict with modern Christianity, but did not under the teaching of the Master.

He who is able to recognize his own weakness, is able to understand the power of virtue — just as the simpleton, when able to respect a wise man, loses his title as a fool.

He who lives in despair and dies in hope, lives to give hope to those who are to die in despair.

Cannot the soul of intelligence be that Law which governs crystallization in minerals, a law of individuality which governs instinct, the milestone of distinct species in the animal: character and personality in man.

I do not seek pleasure. I let it find me.

Forget your kind deeds, so your friends may remind you of them by following your example.

We blindly assume responsibility with eyes upon the reward, balancing lightly the fact that our mountain of ambition is as high as our valley of difficulties and problems is deep. The law of compensation keeps her books perfectly balanced. Though but a dewdrop be absorbed and evaporated, it has its own accounting — by its sediment, which remains: as do man's accomplishments. The hands of the clock themselves mean nothing, though they be studded with diamonds. They may be replaced by a dry twig. For back of them exists a powerful spring governed by a hair-spring, its weakest affinity of impulse which is governed by its compensated regulator, Time. The hands but point to the Past's dead. We have wings, still we dare not fly — just yet.

If a man thinks it is a sacrilege to breathe upon a toad, to him it shall be. As a man thinketh, so is he — but not as he thinketh himself to be.

The man who is selfish, is so ignorant that he cannot see that there is an abundance of everything. The unselfish man knows that there is an exhaustless supply of everything.

Let him who would be heard give his sermons in whispers.

Falsehoods are so subtle that it behooves us to examine the mirror's deformity, rather than to blame its reflection. Neither should we blame a perfect mirror for our own disfigurement.

His foot has reached a precipice, who thinketh himself safe.

This precious electrical force, magnetism, vibrations, subjective consciousness, ether, mental telepathy, intuition, inspiration, illumination, the "voice of the spirit," re-incarnation of thought, "angel voices," the whisperings of God within us, or the honest creation of man's aspiration for Truth — call it cloth, shape, or what you please — will still be the original substance used: the Law of Life and Truth.

He who will not cast a few drops of water upon a dry plant, cannot expect to pluck the flowers.

God does not create a masterpiece just to destroy it. And, as His work is of love and construction, He would never build unless He had a place for this construction. As the soul is all love, we naturally grasp for that inheritance.

Let your imaginary hurts be destroyed by the flame of sleep. The cup of hunger shall be filled for him who will resign himself to the will of his Creator; for there is a way as long as we have eyes, ears, and a tongue, to see, to hear, and to give.

When the gaming season is closed, a hunter is apt to kick his hound about every day. But the first day of the season he will overfeed him and kill him with kindness.

When one starts with all vim, and after a while begins to relax, it is evident that he is not in the right territory—for if the want lasts but a certain time, it proves that the brain, and not the heart is working.

One must feel the sorrow to place the picture into color.

Human faculties are flowing springs of pure water that often dry up for want of use. They may become a destructive flood if turned into one channel by discretion. Endeavor to drink of each, if but one drop, to keep them gently flowing.

Let no spectacular sermon or service control the true good common sense that God gave you. Clarity begins at home, and your prayers should be offered up in your own little bedroom where no one but God and His servants may hear you.

Man can change nothing—except an individuality.

Bear in mind that there is no frown in existence that cannot be destroyed with a smile.

All you really need to make good, is to close your eyes and see nothing but your ambition to do so. Don't lose the thought for one moment, and you will find that every side-track will lead to your point of concentration, just as all tracks lead to a big city.

As we think and act, so we are. Our thoughts leave an indelible mark upon our features, while our actions leave monuments in the graveyards of the memories of others.

If you wish to determine your own value, consider what good you do to those you meet, what value they place upon it, what joy they derive, and what pleasure you have received in giving it: then multiply the result with your own modesty and appreciation.

Just place eight kings in a ditch to dig, and they will accomplish no more than poor Pat, with a pick and shovel. But place them upon their thrones, and where they belong, and you will see some action...

Tears that have evaporated can never be dried by the hand of sympathy. They must be paid for.

It is little credit to a natural-born artist to draw a wonderful picture. There is more credit due to one who is not an artist, and who still draws well.

One must undergo all the anguish of mind that the flesh is heir to, in order to see the wants of others.

We must not judge future events by past experiences.

Let not your feet dance your brain to death.

Some think they must live to eat and to love. Some eat that they may live and be loved. Is it not better to feel that one is born to live, and to understand love, than to think one lives but to die?

Real joys are debts paid in full.

Our desires and ambitions are frames to be filled with that which we lack and which will make us complete. Many of us have unframed art galleries; many of us, pictures to give away, but failing to do so in fear that the frame may outshine the picture, or vice versa.

Curiosity is a mental snare by which curses and blessing seek an outlet.

Some of us mortals give away more grain and fruit than we grow in our field and orchard; and many of us accept more than we need to plant in the Springtime of action.

As jazz music is a mental drug, so is a sweet melody good bread to our hungry bodies.

A mental stimulus is to the body what sunshine is to the flower. Both may grow in shadows: but without distinction of color or beauty.

If you have done all you could, and the world still looks drab—try a little music.

Diplomacy is thrice a virtue when a pleasant smile of forgiveness or tolerance meets and overcomes a grinning sneer of disrespect.

To be affected by the criticism of another, is not only to compliment him, but to admit the question of doubt as to validity of acquirements.

I believe it is far safer to starve on the road to our real want, than to have an attack of gout in but a momentary pleasure that we know is not our own.

He whose one desire to make money, is successful—until he becomes covetous.

Man will live as long as he is able to substitute a mechanical energy for his own, to realize and understand his complexity, to control his animal propensities, and to possess a want. When he is complete, by the amalgamation of every known chemical, life and love which here exists, his mission on earth has been fulfilled.

All that man needs for health, happiness, and prosperity, is hard work under discipline: whether that discipline be self-obligated, through pride, or any other cause. This keeps the well-water of his brain clear, cool and sparkling.

Neglected virtues become burdens of Necessity.

When everything appears undecided, why not visualize your real desires, and govern circumstances, instead of allowing circumstances to govern you? Why not make the dress fit you, instead of trying to make yourself fit into the dress?

An ignorant man displays his emotions in tears: a wise man, in action.

It is the small things that are most important, for they are in the making and can be altered. The big things have already been made, and are permanent.

You who have ever been in fear of Death, and who question Immortality, see before you each day the manifestation of Death, and still you know it not. You, Fathers and Mothers who are atheists, gaze with pride and love upon your baby boys and girls, and are not aware of their loss by Death from Babyhood into Manhood and Womanhood: for they are now within your elements, and the child has passed away. They are called as you are: Man and Woman. And they are called to Death. It is your unreceptive mind which selects and grinds the color that you mix with the Dew of Death upon the brows of those whom you would force into the shadow of Death, the unreal: Manhood, the death of your child; Godhood, the passing of man. Mortality is but a shadow, ill-shaped and deformed; Immortality, the substance upon which the light of God shines in all splendor.

Give more thought to life's tomorrow, to pay for your needs to come, than to the past dead which gives you no return. You can shape the future and offset the past by a perfect masterpiece. You can always patch and repair a broken pitcher — which will make it more valuable through realization and appreciation. Likewise, false pride can be eliminated by asking forgiveness. For greater is he who receives an undeserving blow in silence, than he who strikes one, even though justified.

I would rather trust a thief than an honest man who knows no temptation. Each stumbling block in our way has given us more Prestige, and the right to accept the reward our efforts seek.

Let the man who would be contented, without malice, without envy — let him spin his own web.

One who drifts aimlessly over the waters of inspiration, becomes wrecked upon the shoals of the imagination. Man seeks for truth in every part of this earth, but only at the height of his eyes. He gathers material about him which confuses, hampers and trips his movements, until his progress is uncertain and slow, because of matching his timber to complete the picture of his ideal.

Let him sit himself down and gaze upward, for there he will find Truth, already shaped in all its splendor, as an obedient Servant instead of a pitiless Master.

But we cannot live by bread alone. We must drink water to carry that staff of life through our veins and arteries. As the Master has rightly spoken, "Eat ye and drink of my body and blood." Eat ye the bread of truth, and scatter it to the four parts of the earth by the pure water of deeds and action. What he hath offered thee by birth thou mayest possess in Death.

enLIGHT'NING
FLASHes

I hold this to be self-evident in past history: when communities and nations become crowded by thoughtless, selfish minds, they become over-balanced, lose sight of morals, destroy life and confiscate property. Then after the storm of bloodshed, which relieves the pressure, again comes a new epoch; but toward a higher level of ethics, in search of the arts and sciences destroyed. New and better ones are acquired, lifting man out of the mire and lust and dust of degradation that awakens the soul within to reflect its precepts and principles of God.

— Joseph Sadony

THERE IS GREAT NEED of gathering Thinkers together to lead the non-thinkers. We must give the diamond of Truth a setting of Human Flesh.

GOOD IDEAS, like money should be in circulation to better the world's population.

THE REASON MOST MEN WEAR OUT is because they don't know how to transform the beautiful things around them into energy and enthusiasm.

WE FEAR *for what we doubt in our own.*

THE SAME POWER THAT CREATES is there waiting only for an instant of unbalance to burst its bonds of destruction.

WHEN YOU HERE A SHOT, don't worry if you hear the echo.

WE ARE APT TO FORGET that the leveling of the ocean is not the affair of two drops.

THE BEST TALKER is the man who knows what to say at the right time.

AN IDLE MAN is as useful as a car stalled in traffic without gasoline; and as helpless.

IF YOU DON'T strive for a thing, someone else will use you to do so.

MAN SEES only what he feels, and feels what he longs for.

HE WHO DEFENDS HIMSELF for a virtue he does not possess, adds theft to his sin.

HAPPY IS THE MAN who can make what he needs with what he has.

LIFE is the expression of nature; but love is the expression of God.

THE DANGER in life is to feel too safe — or not safe enough.

THE MAN WHO STARTS a stampede shall be under it if he cannot direct it.

WE LEARN KNOWLEDGE *by success,* but wisdom from failure.

NO ONE CAN FORCE you to break your will but yourself.

THOSE GUILTY of sin are the first to believe a liar.

SOMETIMES WE THINK we become angered by someone else; but it is ourselves.

MAN MAKES WHAT HE CAN to pay for what he can't.

IF PLEASURE *makes you forget,* by sorrow shall you become wise to prevent.

WITH THE SAME NUMBER there are more friends amidst poverty than in wealth.

ARE NOT YOUR LOSSES often due to unexpected profits?

HE WHO MAKES himself a slave to truth becomes a master.

THE MAN WHO KNOWS what he wants is already half way on the road to success in attaining it.

YOUR REAL ENEMY is one you allow in your home with confidence.

HE WHO HOLDS his breath and tongue the longest under waters of discord survives all calamity.

WHY NOT REMEMBER that before a storm it is always quiet and doubtful.

WHEAT will never be a corn, no matter what fertilizer you use for it.

FAULT FINDS FAULT with itself.

WE ARE EACH a missing page of a Book, looking for the Book.

IT IS WELL to learn new swear words so we won't get too used to the old ones.

IF YOU WANT VENGEANCE without regret, don't interfere with God's justice.

SOME OF US FIND a truth, and expect to spend it without having earned or paid for it.

HE WHO SAYS faith is blind, is blind to faith.

WHERE REASON can avoid extremes, logic can control them.

EAT WHEN YOU EAT *and you will sleep when you sleep.*

MAN IS TESTED only by his faith to endure.

ONE NEED NOT express in words what the heart never forgets.

A FOOL acts according to what he is; a wise man according to what he'd like to be.

IF A MAN can sit and listen to birds and enjoy it, he is not very far from God.

THE AUTOGRAPH on a photograph is like the handclasp with the extra grip.

WE FORGET out secret debts, then bemoan the consequences.

EVEN THE VERY GOOD can be selfish to gratify the ego to make others happy.

WHY BELIEVE AN ECHO if you have the voice?

WHEN KINGS dethrone fools, they join them.

STICK TO YOUR JOB or someone else will find yours easier than you thought.

WHEN WE DEPEND IN OUR IMPULSE we are already too late.

GOD BEGRUDGES NO ONE; it is but man who learns to cheat himself by trying to cheat others.

HE WHO HAS FAITH governs his enemies and knows it not.

WISDOM IS NOT what you have learned and forgotten, but what you may use at will.

OBEY THE SIMPLE things of life and the big things will not overthrow you.

HE WHO IS WISE has a right to judge but will not.

A THING LIGHTLY gotten is lightly kept.

A MELODY is being defiled by an instrument that is not in tune, or that has not all the keys.

THEIR OWN FAULTS would be their own discipline.

WHAT HAPPENS HERE *happens all over the world;* but it's not recognized.

AFTER ALL, your success depends mostly on how you have trained your habits.

IF YOU DON'T CULTIVATE the garden of your choice, in love or life, you shall have no fruit of happiness.

ALWAYS BE CAREFUL not to try convince a fool; for he will ask you a question you cannot answer.

HOW MUCH OF YOURSELF do you conceal; then wonder why people ignore you?

THE LORD *never overloads a basket.*

ANYTHING THAT SELLS itself is real.

IT'S NOT WHEN YOU remember somebody, but when they remember you, that is important to you.

HE WHO CLINGS TO LIFE creeps to death.

NATURE TEARS APART all things that insist on not being as well-balanced as she is.

WHEN YOU POSSESS too much power you become blind to it; hence neglect it, only to lose it.

IT'S NO VIRTUE to be clean; it's a necessity.

YOU MAY ACCUSE another unjustly, *but your conscience disagrees.*

WE LOSE THE BEAUTY OF LIFE when we have overeaten our fill of its offerings.

WHY NOT LEARN when you have enough by trying to remember when you had too much?

WE OFTEN MAKE GOOD in what we make people believe us to be.

SOME PEOPLE THINK OF DEATH just to get a kick out of life.

A MAN SHOULD NEVER assume the responsibility that he knows he will never carry.

YOUR WEAKEST ORGAN is the limitation of your strength.

DO NOT SEEK where power ends, but where it is born, to find the source of compensation.

DON'T put a horse's harness on a goat.

THE MAN WHO DOESN'T want much is the happiest one because he isn't disappointed.

THAT MAN IS STRONGEST who has tools and knows how to make use of them.

MAN IS CONSTANTLY hungry, looking for that which will make him hungry.

IT'S THE PERSON WHO REALLY *wants* who has that place waiting for him, to cash in on it.

THE GREATEST excuse for embarrassment: *"Nice day, isn't it!"*

DON'T LET THE BRAIN learn so much it can't use what it's got.

WHO AMONG US SHALL LEAD if we look backward to imitate footprints in the sands already made?

THE MAN WHO FACES NO DANGER of any kind faces a more subtle danger: that of idleness and early old age.

GOD GIVES IS DESIRES, so through them we seek the Giver.

IF A MAN KNEW WHEN to stop talking, he would talk again; but if not, there is a big, black period.

IF YOU LOOK AND LISTEN you may be able to listen and look after the wreck of those who didn't.

TRUTH covers a multitude of virtues.

WHEN WE DEPEND ON OUR IMPULSE, we are already too late.

THE FUNCTIONING OF INTUITION is the fruit of a simple mode of life.

YOU CAN SEE through glasses only when you have them on.

IF CHARACTER GROWS NOT with your wealth, you lose both.

IF ONE MAN does all the fighting, will he not tire himself out, to be ridiculed and condemned?

IF YOU CAN'T BE an actor, then be one of an appreciative audience.

THE MAN WHO KNOWS need never prove it. Actions that follow are self-evidence of the fact.

MANY A MAN loses his temper being forced to live up to what he made people believe he was, but wasn't.

IGNORANT ARROGANCE ALONE is not the sin, but deception added, so false pride too may flourish.

SUFFERING TEMPERS the passions of man; it mellows and tenderizes his bestiality.

PROPHECY is man's heritage, for which he does not grasp, stoning those who do.

WE MUST LEARN not to allow minor influences to control us; we must be conscious of our own propelling force.

CONDEMNATION has *not* the greatest effect to eliminate vice, but careful praise for the remaining virtue.

HE WHO CAN ACCEPT REBUKE with gratefulness will soon learn to wield a scepter with Justice.

HE WHO LEARNS TO SUBDUE his lesser senses, acquires greater power in thought, which is the blossom of the next newborn fruit.

USE SYMPATHY and you won't lose it.

LOVE HAS HOPE where reason dies of starvation.

IT IS NOT ALWAYS a change of mind, but a change of food, that drops the wrench in the gears.

OFTEN WE ABSORB KNOWLEDGE or food not meant for us, and of which, like a stain, we must rid ourselves in order to start anew.

DO YOU NEED A LIFETIME of experience to find out that you were born to have been what you will, and that your bulbs were born before your blossoms?

FAITH IS A LIVING BOOK of future events; history but experience of the dead.

WHEN A MAN ACQUIRES more than he deserves, that moment he loses the value and pleasure of it all.

A MAN BECOMES WISER in the attitude of aspiration than in the realization of his acquired knowledge.

IT'S NOT WHAT you make; it's how you make it, that lives after you. "How" is its soul.

WHAT GOOD ARE LESSONS if you don't learn them?

IF YOU INTEND to climb a high mountain, don't tie yourself to relations who can't.

YOU MUST LIVE long enough to forget your faults.

OFTEN TESTS of worthiness are made through sorrow, depressions and catastrophes. *Cheer up!*

HOW HAVE YOU kept house in that body of yours, to make it think the thoughts you do?

SCRATCH A MAKE-BELIEVE bite long enough and you soon will be obliged to heal it up.

IT IS ONLY TODAY that you may leave your mark. Fail not, good or ill, for others to behold.

THERE IS ALWAYS a future. *Eternity is proof of that.*

PEOPLE SEEM TO FORGET God when most in need of Him.

IT IS ONLY FALSE PRIDE that tries to exhibit a greatness that is not possessed.

THE TRUTH ANSWERS for itself if one is patient.

WHEN IN A MOB it is best to drift along, or you will be trampled upon.

DOES NOT A LITTLE BOY try to steal the apples farthest away, or go to the top shelf for jam?

THE HEAVIEST LOAD KEEPS THE STRAIGHTEST PATH.

PRAYING "*Thy will be done*" does not make it so. You've got to do that.

WHEN YOU DON'T know, be silent so you may.

IF YOU CAN'T walk or talk yourself out of it, think yourself out of it.

YOU MAY SEE your virtues; but the question is, do you feel them?

SO FEW SEEK THE FUTURE that those who do are alone.

OUR OWN SINS judge us; our own virtues forgive us.

HE WHO TALKS too much is baiting a trap for a hungry man who, when caught, starves to death.

IT IS ONLY A FOOL who is ever ready to call others one.

THE TRUTH is no better for your telling it, but you are better for trying to be a part of it.

IS THE OPINION of a fool more valuable than the oath of a hypocrite?

WHICH IS GREATER: *an honest failure* or a cheater's success?

A BIG MAN can be simple and small; but a small man can't afford to be big, for then he won't live long.

CAN GOD TRUST *you with the confidence of a sinner?*

IF YOU ARE NOT in touch with God above the clouds, then you are under the dominion of man.

WHY DO SO MANY good ears listen to evil tongues, then wonder what blinded them?

A MAN WITH BRAINS on a tension is hurt by idle and useless things.

SWEETNESS can be surpassed only by a pinch of salt or a drop of bitter.

MANY USE THE COIN of sorrow to pay for lasting happiness.

WITHOUT A FULCRUM a crow-bar isn't worth a darn.

WHEN A MAN DWELLS on what he has done, he shows what he can't do, or he would have done it.

YOU TAKE WHAT YOU GET, ah yes, but you don't get what you take.

LITTLE THINGS look best in small mirrors, and are more appreciated.

AN IDEAL is a negative. Make it a positive. You can.

IF YOU FAIL to discover new truths, repeat old ones that have been forgotten.

IF YOU DON'T keep your place, someone will take it. *Can you object?*

MAN MAKES MORE effort to steal a thing than to pay for it. *Why?*

THE MORE WISE you are, the greater your personal responsibility to impart it.

TRY TO BE as good a loser as you are a winner, and you will feel more safe.

WHAT THE MIND is able to conceive, within the bounds of reason and common sense, may be realized.

MANY TIMES grief is a key to happiness, and failure a key to success.

IN SWATTING A FLY, you know, we often hit ourselves with more vigor than we intended.

IT IS YOUR OWN FAULT if you make yourself a prisoner by borrowing the rut of another.

IF YOU DEPRIVE YOURSELF of your duty by relieving another of his, your sin is two-fold.

YOU CAN CONVINCE a fool by just making a fool of him.

WHAT MAN HAS FREEDOM who does not seek bondage?

IT IS NOT ALL in how you live, but how you die, and why?

ONE WHO CANNOT TAKE his own medicine has no right to give it to others.

IT IS WELL TO REMEMBER that the corn on your foot hurts only you.

NO BIG SHEPHERD ignores the little shepherd as long as there is one lamb left.

THE MAN WHO DEALS IN FAITH has hope to give away.

ARE NOT MEETINGS the beginnings of separations?

WHERE ARE YOU GOING so fast to waste your time?

WHEN CHRIST SAID, "*Feed my lambs*", He did not mean "Shear their wool and eat lamb chops."

IT IS GOOD to have respect tested by the temperature of a fool.

ENJOY YOURSELF A LITTLE every day because it's getting later than you think.

DON'T EXPECT cleanliness, order and respect where there is no pride.

WHY NOT SHOW people what they have got, instead of your picture of *Micky Mouse?*

THEY WERE ACTING a thing that was true; but not true in their acting.

HIS FALSE PRIDE and his own deception changed the name of God to *Satan.*

MAN ...KES HIMSELF believe he is better than anything else; and by t.. belief makes it come true.

IF YOU DON'T use your head, you'll wear out your feet. Which do you need most?

WE LET OUR MINDS grow indefinitely, until we believe our wrong is right.

THERE IS NOT A MAN who is not interested in what concerns himself, either for or against him.

HE WHO STEALS the truth binds himself to it.

CAN WE SAY that the visible world is the perishable explanation of the eternal truth?

HE WHO CALLS FOR HELP before danger, warns the wolf when to attack.

A MAN who has to live on the past is a scavenger.

WE OFTEN FIND the truth when too late to use it; friends when we lose them; love at the door of the grave.

GOD GAVE EACH a little flame and a gallon of water, so each can come home under his own steam.

TO OVERCOME MONOTONY is progress.

WHERE HAS YOUR ENEMY gone when you have made a friend of him?

TRY TO FORGET yourself, so you will not remember the ailments you haven't got.

IF YOU CAN THINK YOURSELF what you want to be, then you already are.

IF YOU are a butter and egg man, don't forget that you must have cows and chickens.

EVEN IN A ROTTEN APPLE there is a seed that can prod... orchard; so why throw it away? an

ANYTHING YOU DO is only as important as you make it, so far as you are concerned.

DOES NOT YOUR NEW responsibility often blind you to the old, normal joy: the simplicity that once was?

THERE IS NOTHING more truthful than the truth.

LET A DICTATOR beware when two great men agree in his community.

YOU MAY GENERALLY know what a man is worth according to what he does in his idle moments.

IF YOU HAVE A FEAR OF FALLING, see how far you can travel, not how high you can climb.

THE SWORD IS JEALOUS because of the arm that is weak.

ONE WHO ENGENDERS HATE by the sword of selfish criticism dies by the sword of justice.

WHY NOT ELIMINATE doubt and give your hope a chance to strengthen your faith in yourself?

THERE IS ONLY ONE WAY for a man to lose a real friend, and that is for him to lose himself.

A "BIG SHOT" is a little shot trying to be a big shot.

A THIEF steals from himself his clear conscience.

HE WHO HATES ANOTHER borrows from his victim, fear.

MAKE MEN fear your honesty, respect your understanding, and love your kindness.

A DOG ONLY BARKS; it requires man's reason to know why.

148

THE CURE for idle misery is labor's contentment.

HE WHO HOLDS HIS FIRE has always death to deal out.

THE WAGES of happiness are found in frugality and thrift.

EVERYBODY WANTS to wear diamonds but they don't want to dig for them.

WHAT YOU WANTED YESTERDAY is dead today.

IF YOU ARE GUILTY of anything don't look for powder or dynamite with a match.

NO MATTER WHO the pagan may be I shall still respect his God.

THERE IS SOMETHING suspected and expected of every man.

SOME PEOPLE won't like what they could like, so they look for what they can't like if they have it.

WE OFTEN SAVE our lives by the sacrifice of what we lost.

HOW EASY IT IS to get courage; and with courage, how easy it is to succeed!

IF ONE DOESN'T KNOW what to give, he has nothing to receive.

YOU ARE UNWORTHY of protection if you do not do your part, as weak as it may be, to prevent.

BE PATIENT! Eternity teaches us never to count.

THE MAN WHO ACTS with vulgarity has no respect for respect.

NEGLECTED VIRTUES become burdens of necessity.

GOD WAITS to win back His own flowers as gifts from man's hands.

FORTUNATE IS THE MAN who knows his own faults and does not defend them.

NO ONE CARES to dry his face on a wet towel.

YOU GET JUST what you give; and what you take, you pay for. No man is exempt.

THE DIAMOND in the ring is safe only according to the wearer.

HE WHO TAKES NO advantage of others is doubly welcome by all, even a vicious dog.

WITH HONOR comes responsibilities, and with responsibilities comes worry if you don't relax.

IF YOU CAN'T lengthen your life by years, do so by activity.

DON'T HAVE such respect for a person unworthy that it will make you lose respect for yourself.

IF YOU THINK you have time to burn, why not wait until after you die before blistering your friends.

BE SURE that your gratefulness is honest gratitude, and not a bait.

"I NEVER HURT ANYBODY." *No. But you don't save anybody either.*

IF YOU ACCEPT flattery, and thank the flatterer you give a receipt for counterfeit money.

ALL LIFE IS A LABOR until we love to labor, and then it is play.

THE LORD POINTS where the water is; man must make a pump.

EVERYTHING IS STUBBORN — when dirty.

BLESSED IS HE who knows what to do — and does it.

IT IS ONLY A FOOL who can be discourteous.

IN THE WORLD OF DISCORD EVERY deed done must be accounted for by him who did it.

PEOPLE WHO THINK OUT LOUD are just as shallow as what they say.

POWER is for him who is strong enough to harness it, and wise enough to use it properly.

A MAN WHO IS ALIVE can no more prove he is alive than a man who is dead can prove he is dead.

WE LIVE WITHIN THE TRUE LAW only when we are not aware of anything else.

GOD PUTS INTO the brain of man the value of his existence. Thus a fool treads where angels fear.

IF YOU HAVE something to give, where did you get it?

MOST OF US TRY to labor when we are old, but can't; most of us can, when young, but we won't.

IF YOU WANT to respect yourself, look into the mirror every day and see if you can.

HAVE YOU EVER TRIED *to* make each eye do its own seeing? Try it.

WHEN YOU ARE virtuous you can sin; but when you are not virtuous, you are a sinner.

WHERE IT IS FOLLY to be wise, it must be wise to be foolish.

DO YOU POSSESS your wife's body, heart and mind, respect, love and soul? Someone does.

FAITH REMOVES MOUNTAINS by removing you to where there are no mountains.

I HAVE NEVER YET seen love forced, sold or bought; but I have seen it exchanged.

ONE MAY ASSUME a new environment by what memory has recorded, but find reality not the same.

ONE FORGETS TO PLAY when one stimulates ambition too far.

THEY ALL WANT a clear conscience, and to have a clear conscience they've got to do some camouflaging.

OFTEN TRUTH is what dreams are made of.

MEMORY HAS A WAY to shape dreams without restrictions or tinsel. *Then we wonder why.*

SOME WELL-TO-DO MEN who were once poor, still believe, think and act it.

THE BIRTH OF THE SOUL is when it bursts the bonds of materialism.

CAN THERE BE any inheritance in fame?

TO PRAY is to listen to a spiritual message for one's good.

INVINCIBLE IS HE whom you cannot harm by criticism or revenge.

IF YOU ARE HOMELY, dress up your best; but if you are beautiful, dress simply.

SOME MEN work for money; other men make money work for them.

IDLENESS and good food invite the most vicious habits of mankind.

A STRANGE, NEW GUN is dangerous at both ends, even if not loaded.

THE ONE WHO SAYS, "*I am the Dictator!*" isn't.

IF YOU KNOW what might be, your intuition will tell you what will be.

A FULL CAPACITY in nature demands delivery, or the penalty of forfeiture.

WHAT'S WORTH SAYING need not be said, but should be remembered.

152

' God so he may find Him within himself.

.w the death of desire, where faith doubts and
.ır.

.LD'S BATTLES are lost by the efforts to win them.

UP your dynamite without knowing what it was.

.₤W BROOM sweeps no cleaner than an old one. It depends on the hands that grasp it. It is the ambition of him who sweeps.

A MAN WHO TALKS TOO MUCH *has already* neglected his day's labor.

EPITAPH: For the lack of ambition to blind his fear he remained a coward.

THERE IS STILL more hope for fools that are than those that were.

LET THE TROUBLES of others burn out your own.

THE VALUE of a pitcher is known only after it is broken; and then it is useless.

WHEN YOU FLATTER your friend you strengthen his vanity and adulterate his virtues.

NO ONE CAN TELL how cold it is until he can tell how warm it was.

A FOOL may find fault with you; but are you wise enough to recognize your own?

THE MAN WHO PLAYS FAIR and loses, wins.

THE MAN WHO CAN lose himself in his work will find himself in his play.

IT'S A CLEVER MAN who can force a favor upon you when you needed none to be indebted to him.

IF YOU HAVE something to give away, and don't, then you.

THE MAN WHO IS remembered most, was most.

WHEN GOD can trust you, you are apt to live up to it.

HE WHO CRITICISES the good bread offered, is not hungry—but soon will be.

TAKE A LITTLE, improve a little, and leave a little, to be remembered a little.

SOME MEN who want to be good, try so hard that they become bad.

MEN ARE CHOSEN who are best able to do what is best, under the law of moral compensation.

THE MAN WHO GIVES of himself lives the length of its value even though he be dead.

WHEN A MAN ADMITS he knows nothing, he is measuring what he doesn't know.

IF YOU HAVE AN IDEA and wait too long to express it, it dies. Most intentions die before they are born.

YOU ARE YOUNGER today than you ever will be. Make use of it for the sake of tomorrow.

YOUR FEAR makes you lose. Knowing this, you can win.

YOU CANNOT LOSE what is yours. Whether you go higher or lower you will land where you fit.

WHAT BARGAIN have you made with your digestive organs that you are so abusive of them?

THE MAN WHO LIVES within the chamber of licentious thoughts must expect to pay its rent.

YOU ARE USING ten dollars' worth of bait for ten cents of fish.

SINCE LOSING YOUR MONEY haven't you found what you thought you lost long ago?

YOU NEED NEVER BE A PRISONER, not even in forced solitary confinement, unless you strangle your will.

VERY FEW MEN have ever died of hard work; most of them die of worrying over it.

SOMETIMES there is a greater reward in failure than in success.

IF YOU THINK NOT, then you will do twice: you will pay up and still be in debt.

THE MAN WHO THINKS he is being persecuted, is; but usually it is only by himself.

HE WHOM YOU CONVINCE against his will, will curse you for knowing his weakness.

NEVER TRY to beat a fool; for when you do, you're a bigger one.

THE TRAGEDY IS that most couples don't know the law of love and companionship.

OUR FEAR OF IT gives birth to what would never happen if we forgot it.

AS LONG AS HALF of the people are not taught how to live, the other half know what to live on.

HE WHO HOLDS HIS TEMPER is greater than the man who provokes it.

YOU CAN'T convince a fool, but you can fool a wise man.

MANY A GOOD IDEA has been hid under a bum hat.

WHY STOP in the middle of the desert just because you got through the jungle?

THE TIME TO BE CAUTIOUS is when you don't want to want.

ONE WHO CAN TOUCH the depths of sorrow and emerge with a smile, is worthy of the greatest joy.

IF YOU HAVE NO HOPE, then create a Want, to give birth to hope.

FAR BETTER REVEAL the truth than criticize the lack of it, for want of it yourself.

A PARROT may teach another all it knows; still neither one knows what he is talking about.

IS IT ENOUGH to find gold, or love? Or must we make use of it and preserve it to live?

YOUR STRENGTH is judged by those who love you; your reputation by those who don't.

IF YOU CAN'T find the truth direct, check up on lies.

LIVE AND LET LIVE — but beware of the man who laughs.

A PERSON who does not improve things is not improving himself.

IF A MAN HAS SOMETHING better than you have, give him credit. Take off your hat to him — and steal his.

MANY PEOPLE LET the left hand of vice destroy the right hand of virtue.

THE RICH MAN who takes out of the poor box loses what he has.

THE WORLD is as bad and deformed as the glasses we use.

LIKE THE FRUIT TREE man must bear or be buried.

THERE IS JUST as much of a trick in waiting for something to come, as in doing it.

THE REASON *eternity* is known and tasted by those in love is because they pay no attention to time.

MOST OF US don't know how or when to grasp; some don't know how and when to let go.

IT IS MORE IMPORTANT sometimes to sustain your reputation than to make one.

TO THE MAN who can ignore a thing it is not.

SOME PEOPLE TAKE NARCOTICS to forget something they will never forget.

OUR BAD HABITS make us prisoners, and our false pride is the jailer that keeps us there.

WE ALWAYS lose sight of what we've got, in our efforts to obtain what we haven't got.

IF YOU CAN'T THINK it out, you can't act it out.

IF YOU HAVE A BIG LOAD don't stop, or you may have to hire another load to start up again.

THERE MAY NOT ALWAYS be smoke where there is fire, but there is always fire where there is smoke.

THE COMPLETION OF LOVE carries one into the presence of God.

SIT DOWN AND MEDITATE: from within, a new world shall be born, in place of what you are forced to accept.

OFTEN WHEN YOU become blind and stubborn, you are not a leader; neither a follower.

YOU ARE ASKED for the Hand of God, to be led; so why do you lead Him?

157

IF YOU LOSE YOURSELF serving men God will find you to be served.

THE WORLD NEEDS MEN of quality, self-appointed, who know and know that they know how to meet problems for those too blind who use telescopes and microscopes to see with procrastination while starving to death today.

PERIODICALLY IN HISTORY the ground of man's mind is plowed under, everything apparently uprooted into uncertainty. How else shall the old habits of thought be broken up to clear the way for a new epoch?

NOW BEGINS an epoch of permanent constructiveness after destructive fermentation of insincere human emotions fertilized in virgin soil by the ill-gotten gains of selfish greed, strengthening newborn virtue by dead vices.

GOD HAS been giving real men their best chance now to prove manhood and still exist. A test has been made, and is being made, by Nature's game of elimination which always precedes a new era. The kettle boiling over always separates the impure from the pure, so that everyone has an opportunity to make good who has previously failed.

THE WORLD is waiting for facts that can be eaten for today, and used for tomorrow. All men and women are beginning to wake up. Many have already awakened. New plans, systems, organizations, fraternities, methods, styles have been and are springing up, and will spring up from every State; not alone to economize, and to prevent waste, but to awaken Art, Music, Science, Literature, Fraternalism and that neighborly, loving constitution "for the other fellow."

This had to come. If we do not let go of one bead of the Rosary, we shall never reach the Cross.

WHO AMONG US, the living, today are worthy to lead, to admonish and to judge morals, deeds and actions? Are they of the wealthy who have not earned it? Those who have, but are not able to use it judiciously? The very poor who have nothing to enable them to judge its value? The philosopher who may know, but be influenced only by his own sacrifice? He of a tribe that has not been allowed voice for centuries, but a slave to the stronger who accepted and became stronger in physical power only, where might was right? Or should not that hand of progress accept one finger from each, as a complete Hand, of the viewpoint of the Human Race: so that the human family on earth may be complete according to credit due in labor, love and understanding?

Sadony at his desk

Pine Needles

From The Valley of the Pines

Happy is the man
Who knows neither his own weight, strength
Nor destiny.
But whose emotions awaken
At every turn of the road.
Who enjoys a lifelong time of appreciation,
With every aspiration guarded.
Who spends his interest on inheritance,
And at death's door finds his capital
Of soul untouched.
That man is a man
Who follows in the shadow of the Master

The man who has a purpose in life,
Who lives in silence,
Who visualizes no other,
Will surely attain it.
He is poised on his toes,
He is ever ready to spring,
His patience and silence in waiting are his greatest activity.

Don't let your memory of past failure or discord
Swerve you from your set purpose of possibilities still unborn.
Forget by remembering future possibilities.
Think only of success,
And not only will you feed it,
But you will starve failure.
You can deform education and music,
But simplicity of purpose is like a large reservoir
With water gates made of concrete and steel
To allow only enough water to pass through to harmonize
With Nature's progress of production and consumption,
That it may neither run dry,
Nor become a flood to destroy.

The man who labors in silence and darkness
Possesses more power
Than he who holds high his hand in broad daylight
And proclaims his intentions.

In everything that appears good, you may find bad.
A gun may protect you, also kill you.
A knife has its use for or against you.
Electricity may be your servant, and also destroy you.
Food can give health, also sickness.
Small-pox virus may make you immune,
But too much will cause your death.
Too much of any good thing will destroy your equilibrium, your
physical poise, or mental balance.
Your body is supposed to represent the earth
In all its parts, harmoniously, in beauty and strength;
The most enduring, artistic, graceful, compact, complete mansion
Where the soul may live as the King of the Earth.

If you play fair,
Regardless how you lose, you win.
You may have a poor partner to make you lose today;
But tomorrow you will have a better partner than you are,
Who will win for you what you lost today
Just because you were or would have been a good loser,
Having done the best you could.

The more strings you find to the human harp,
The greater your song of emotions, happiness, and success.
So search for each string hidden.
See to it that it is tuned correctly.
Then you may hear every song ever sung.
You need but to listen,
And each mental faculty will vibrate its secret of life.
Listen only, for your voice can only repeat,
And you will know why the wise men are often silent.
They are listening to the voice of growth, life, and God's message
Do you envy the success of others;
Complain at your misfortune?
If so, bear in mind that there is no living thing
That must not work in darkness of the mines.
Even the Embryo of the life within its prison walls of shell or flesh
The roots of flowers and trees,
Man in the dark ages of ignorance.
He digs up his metal for swords and plowshares, locks and powder
If he fails to wear a crown that fits him,

It was then like the tree that complained that it failed to blossom,
Because it did not labor among its roots to produce them,
Let alone the fruits longing to follow the blossoms unto life.

When God can trust His creation
He will place in Man's hand
A most precious power
To create what he will.
And when Man realizes this
He will have burned out
All inclination to do wrong.

Often men think they are making great progress
Because their feet carrying big loads run swiftly;
But are blind to the fact that they are in a revolving
Squirrel cage getting nowhere;
And the man sincere. working daily, sees no progress
Because he is traveling on the large ship of Progress, unaware.

It is not enough that we write a letter.
We must have the address, buy a stamp and mail it.
It is not enough to love.
We must repay.
Not enough to earn money.
We must spend it well.
Not enough to pray.
We must give prayer muscle to attain.
It is not enough to possess a steel bar to make a compass,
We need a prayer of magnetism to discern.
A prayer is but to tune in so we may realize a duty of Nature.
To show us the land-marks to obey a law
That we might live right, according to that which
Created our being and consciousness.
Our prayer is but a hammer to the chisel,
Hope to faith, internal light in the dark nights of doubt and despair.
It is the birth of hope
That faith may lead us to its realization,
To admit a supreme Being,
A law greater than our conception,
To recognize a power we must obey,
A wall of obedience; a recipe,

Directions to attain that which will fill a vacuum,
A felt want to complete an Ideal.

Calamities and misfortunes are but brakes applied
To your freight train going down your mountainside;
Or sand thrown across the path of your sled that has no brakes,
In order to slow up your speed,
So you may reason why and where you are going to land,
Before it is too late.
Nature uses this means of vaccination while still in your prime
And strong enough to avoid and withstand the vicissitudes of life.

Don't condemn a fool for lack of wisdom.
He is at least contented,
While a man of wisdom may be happy,
But the law of adjustment gives him a personal responsibility,
Which prevents what constitutes the contentment of a fool.

Try to remember everything
On your journey up the mountain of life,
So that when you glide coasting down
You may know what to do, and avoid,
In order to complete your life successfully.

If your mind is not in your exercise,
Your heart not in your love,
You are but putting a losing, useless drain upon your energy —
A false hope in your Ideals.

No man need envy another.
Nature has so constructed its laws
That each man may create and live in a world of his own;
And as with the stars of heaven,
Need injure none by contact, though living in one mansion.

Do not fear to do wrong.
Fear rather that you might fail
To do good.
Do not think you have lost,
What you have never found.
For there is nothing ever lost,

Or ever found.
If we have "found,"
It belongs to another.
If we have "lost,"
It was never ours.

We still have more to learn
Of the rooms of man's mind,
To find the doors leading to that religious ecstasy,
The mystery, the frenzy of the aborigines,
The bliss of divinity felt by martyrs and saints,
The hypnotic power of our professional men
All still in its infancy.
Who shall dare to ridicule or challenge unknown facts,
The vehicle which led the human race to absolute facts,
The few that we have,
Still, self-evident.
Can we not be charitable enough
To believe men sincere in their own honest convictions?
Time will prove a greater power in man's mind
Than we have thus far admitted.

You may assume vows before the eyes of men,
But the vows before the eye of your soul
Are more sacred and binding by your conscience than any others.

Every man and woman is placed in a melting pot of life,
Sorted according to his ambition.
The fire of experience either burns them to dross
Or purifies to achieve.
He who possesses character need not fear the flame of elimination;
But those who have cause to fear are but returned
To whence fear lost confidence.
They are depreciated for their assumed credit.
For every plant there grows an affinity
Upon which it may live and thrive,
Be it food or love, to destroy or to save.

In trying to make the world better
By making others obey your will and opinion,
Why not make yourself obey

And let the example show its effect?
And each be a captain of his own ship,
So that the human inclination of the "masses" will do likewise
Steering it safely,
Instead of one mortal trying to do so,
Which is impossible.

Whenever you wish to do something,
No matter what it might be,
Think twice —
The day thought and the night thought,
The result to others,
And the result to yourself.
It will astonish you
What an interesting game you may play
During the rest of your life.

It's time ill spent
To labor for the approbation of acquaintances.
In the final reckoning
You shall receive only criticism
For your pains.
The Evil will condemn your efforts,
Because of your patience with good.
And the Good
Will question
Your pity for Evil.

The time a person really suffers tortures is when he has sympathy for those in pain or sorrow.

Try to learn to think what you want to think, that will bring happiness. Then see the attitude of your emotions, your faith and the results. Thoughts come first; regret or action next, and if the latter, happiness results.

Do you think your body is the only place you can live in? If so, tell me where you are in your dreams, far from home?

Half of the time you did not mean what you said to hurt. It was but habitual, and you felt the stronger of the two. So go easy not to let things slip over the tongue that you may regret and never make good.

Is not the simple life the best
After all?
Is there much to be gained
By responsibilities and fame?
Do they strengthen our hearts and love?
Or do they honor our egotism
And inflame our pride?
The more we acquire,
The more a slave to circumstances
We are apt to become —
Until we may not call our soul our own.

If I offer you an epigram you cannot digest,
Then I have given you something of value.
And you find that your sharp knife
Of discrimination
Is still in your hand,
And rust is not blunting the cutting edge.
Real joys are debts paid in full.

Don't try to think with your brain when that brain is not normal —
Causing thoughts not normal.
Is it not like a tired body which cannot raise an arm?
Why expect a tired brain to do more?
Surely you ought to know when a straight line is made crooked,
As well as when a circle is made straight,
And realize that if you know the difference,
The knowing is proof of an inborn, independent justice,
A knowledge of a moral law,
A conscience of set rule, wrong and right, top or bottom, cold or hot
Our own law of cause and effect adjusts our judgment
As to what is the cause, and what is the effect,
Whether standing on our feet, or walking on our hands.

Often when you turn off the light, you find you can't sleep. Well, then keep the light on and try to keep your eyes open. You fall asleep, because you are seeing with your eyes. But when dark, you see with

your thoughts, and that keeps you awake. I've tried, and I'm no better
than you are; and perhaps no worse.

No man can hope in one life
To complete great achievements.
He can expect to accomplish
Only that which is himself.
He may build the greatest ship
But fail to see it launched.
Plan the greatest city
For his children to build and complete.
Paint the greatest picture
For age to illuminate.
But he may build a ladder
Which by the aspiration of his Soul
Will reach into heaven.

Don't despair at your slow growth as roots of an oak tree.
The more slowly you grow, and the more sure of yourself,
The greater will be your tree that will be supported
By your long development.
Don't mind those plants that mature overnight
They eat, and live only for the next day.
Do you expect so short a life?
It requires but twenty-one days to hatch a chicken egg.
What about a goose, and how long does it live?
You must pay the fiddler by the hour,
Not by the tune.
Are not the limbs of the coming oak,
Yes, even the leaves, predestined as to their respective
Position on that tree
Within that small acorn, as the nerves and arteries
Within the embryo of man
To designate its species?

Does thought give you pleasure?
If not, is not anticipation a part of the realization?
And if true, why not create more thought of happiness
To hasten the ambitions of your heart?

Your strength is judged by those who love you,
Your reputation by those who don't.

Periodically in history the ground of man's mind is plowed under,
everything apparently uprooted into uncertainty. How else shall the
old habits of thought be broken up to clear the way for a new epoch?

He is only successful who, after having attained his goal, remembers
his friends who see in him the same friend of old, whose success has
not stained nor embittered him.

A doctor can help you live
As long as there is still a tension on your main spring;
But if that has run down,
No matter how good the works and jeweled settings,
Don't expect him to do what God and Nature has forbidden.
The main spring absorbs that which it gives up,
Regardless of the value of the works,
Which in turn must be kept in good condition
Or there will be that pull of the spring still there
To work, escape, or be placed in another
Rundown clock in good repair
All created to tell us of wasted time
That might have been used in knowing all these things
To lengthen opportunities and happiness.
See a good jeweler occasionally,
If your clock goes too slow;
And a minister of the gospel to get the correct time,
And a doctor to set and clean the work.

If you have made a mistake,
Why not backtrack
Just to convince yourself how it happened,
And save a lot of good wasted self-pity
Making your next mistake in thinking people believe your alibi.

Do you believe,
Because you can afford the life of ease,
That it exempts you from labor,
When labor is so essential for physical strength,
To support the mental wealth by its personal responsibility?

If your eyes fail to wake up your soul
By the display of beauty and art,
Your ears, as sensitive as they may be,
Shall be deaf to all music, melody, and words of love;
For seeing, hearing, tasting, and feeling enter different doors,
But into one room only.

It is useless to worry over what cannot be helped.
And what cannot be helped calls for action,
Not worry.
Worry saps vitality.
And renders one unfit for the action
Necessary to make conditions better.

When you think yourself greater
Than your brother man,
Remind yourself of those things
That you did ungraciously and unwell.

Prayer is but a cup to be filled,
An appeal to the unknown, and not an order,
Not a demand for that which we ourselves may do or reason.
It is to tune in, to strengthen hope unto faith,
That patient path that leads to what we prayed for,
A telescope to see; a microscope to discern.

If you have a just reason to become angry,
And keep it under control,
You punish your enemy.
But if you give way to it,
Your anger punishes you.

How often have we not been let down, forsaken, depressed in spirit.
But how do we know that it isn't a test of our sincerity of purpose and
worthiness in overcoming adversity when in our power to do so? Has
this not perhaps been given us as an honor of trust by Him who gave
us life and individuality to rise above it all and achieve reward for
efforts made?

It's not what you do when you are busy that counts most. It is what
you do when you are idle that makes or breaks you.

If you fail to make good, and do not know why,
Have you ever stopped to think
That it might be a childish dream of fear, petrified,
Which still remains with you, unconsciously?
Have you ever stopped to think that our anger and disappointment
Magnify more by our unreasonable selfish imagination
Than that which first caused our anger,
So easy then to forgive,
Until we have added our own subtle poison of
Disappointment or false pride?

Most of us are becoming blind to today's opportunity
Which might shape tomorrow's success.
Instead, we but hope for tomorrow's success;
And fail because of today's neglect.

The spirit of serving is becoming
To the high
As well as the lowly.
But dignity belongs to him
Who is able to uphold it.

Few of us think real thought.
We only think we think,
It is all Vanity in new forms.
One must be alone to think,
Uninfluenced by the world's desires.

Don't be too hasty to collect your first week's wages;
Neither expect a silver cup at your first attempt.
Be glad for the attempt.
Victory and silver cups follow always.
If you still have faith after your first three prayers were answered
You may be sure your recommendation is being placed on record.
To deliver goods on credit.

There is a limit to man's power of reasoning.
He may be finally able to complete
A jig-saw puzzle,
In a fashion according to the
Number of blocks he has found

Through his efforts to excel.
But in his youth it makes no difference
What block he chooses first,
In his attempt to solve the Unknown,
He will but reach a plane of incompleteness,
Until each block of life's problems
Has been found, and properly placed.
And when he reaches that point of evolution,
Man's understanding may, perhaps,
Partake somewhat of completeness and universality.

Daily contact with an enemy results in the enemy being despised.
But if he is avoided, he creates another weapon to hurt in his absence.
The farther removed the more horrible the cry of the battlefield.
Problems and misfortunes are blessings of immunity
To oblivion and failure.
They awaken and exercise a sluggish brain.
They strengthen faith and hope born in the Soul.
But if sorrows and calamities go by unnoticed —
If no lesson has been learned, then a life has been in vain.
How can we enjoy without having known sorrow?
How can we know sorrow without joy?
Sympathy is born in sorrow.
Appreciation often dies in joy.
But the memory of both sorrow and joy awakens faith,
Hope and charity, consideration, kindness and love.

There are sorrows which time alone can cure
By what light we find appertaining to Eternity.
When we deliberately lose one eyelid, we do not destroy light,
But only shut it from our own view:
That light which but reflects itself, lends its truth,
Brings out the soul of that which it touches.
So keep your eyes open.
At best they see but dimly.

The last stroke of the bell
Tells the time.
The others tell only part of the truth.

Live right and you will act right.
Act right, and you will have to think right.

Things are only beautiful when you are in tune with them
If you are not, then tune yourself in.
It may be your fault.

To improve the future,
Review the past.
Our sorrows are receipts for debts paid.
Our good deeds are negotiable checks.

The see-saw of life must be kept balanced,
For such is the law.
But ever upon the end that is high up
Will I throw my weight
For the sake of your Soul.
If you have lifted high
And dragged down the clouds from
Where they belong,
And walk the earth, half-dazed
In a spiritual mist,
While the good feet of your body
Dangle helpless,
Do not think me cruel
If I demand red blood where red blood is needed.
And if I tell you
That well-prepared food, and care of the body,
Are as important for the Soul
As are thoughts of God.

It is the value you place on your interest for tomorrow that gives birth and strength to your hopes and verifies your faith and leaves no grounds for fear, apprehension or sorrow.

Who is wrong when a man is accused of a wrong that he sincerely believes was right, and is then called a liar because it was a lie to another, but not so to him who honestly believed it to be the truth? Are they not both to blame for not understanding each other?

In the name of Charity and Love,
Give your surplus profits in your youth,
So they may be returned to you
In your old age
As necessities.

If you would be safe from
Superstition and spiritual fanaticism
Remain near the shore
Of the stream of life,
Where reason may direct you.
When in the water,
Not to go beyond your depth,
Not to drift upon the running stream,
And to hold you,
When upon the shore,
From wandering out into the desert.

Man is tested only by his faith to endure.

In human experience,
Perhaps the most precious time lost,
The greatest tortures,
The most tears shed,
The greatest cruelties,
Wars and bloodshed,
Have been endured and committed
In the name of a man-shaped God
And (what irony!) called Love.
Humanity has shaped and clothed Him.
Which is as impossible as for a new-born Babe
To support its father by its understanding.
Why? When? And where?
An understanding mind knows that God exists.
Whether we are in His likeness,
Or will be in centuries to come,
Or perhaps at the close of our perfection,
Or never —
It does not matter.
The great problem that has been,
Is, and ever will be before us,

Is to learn, not what to love —
But how?

No one will deny facts, unless he has a subtle purpose to use opportunities for selfish purposes. Truth is self-evident and needs no support. It supports itself. And if the pillars of a structure are lies, it will but collapse. Still, the spirit of true support is ever present, so that a new permanent structure shall rise from the ashes and dust of falsehood. There are ever present health germs to continue life, even among death germs. That is the law of adjustment, compensation and growth, the manifestation of life.

All that matters most to man is back of his eyes, and there he flounders in the dark, thinking he thinks a thought, but unaware of the origin of that thought, or of its fruits; "Imagining" things without the slightest conception of the power and mechanism that he is using.

Do you ever hear or enjoy birds singing?
If not, your judgment is lopsided.
Even your art is deformed,
Or you may be stone deaf.
If the latter, your eyes should hear their song;
For even in a "Depression",
Nature sings her song of praise,
Except man, its master, who learns to forget.

I believe it is best to carry a little good timber, and only a few first-class tools — having them always ready at hand — than to carry many tools and much timber to hew and shape. Accept from the store of knowledge only that which you actually need in life's battle, and no more, or you will be too heavily weighted. It is not the knowledge that is acquired that matters. It is how it is used.

All life is a labor
Until we love to labor,
And then it is play.

He who is humble with simplicity has a right to it
Only when he has the primitive strength to convince;
Because a coward may be humble, through fear;

A fool, simple through ignorance.
But it requires strength to burn dynamite slowly.

Never defend a fault but prune the evil plant.
To admit it is to pull it up by the roots.
And if you do, you will have enough strength of character
To profit by it.
Do not let your thoughts run idle.
Try to keep them in a channel to clothe them so they may live
Within themselves and bear fruit.

Do not be so egotistical as to think
That God has neglected to pick
Someone to fill your place
When you leave this earth,
No matter what your responsibilities
Or what throne you have sat upon.

The good you have done can no more be destroyed
Than an atom annihilated.
You might release power into a new form
But you cannot destroy it
Just because you cannot see it after its transformation,
It is still in existence
As well as our unkind deeds.

Why fight or dispute when there is nothing to fight about?
For the truth still remains, regardless of the outcome.
And truth defends itself.
And the man who fights, loses — even if he wins.

He who lives by the sword
Must not expect mercy when it is shattered.
But he who gives mercy
Need never ask it.

He who carries the atmosphere of nobility about him,
Heals the multitudes merely by his presence.
He frees — never enslaves.
Will-power repels.
He who uses will-power to enslave others

Finds himself enslaved.
The greatest and noblest quality is kindness,
Kindness to all living things.
Life is an individual unfoldment
Which necessitates the constant observance
Of our thoughts, words, deeds.
No other one is so much concerned with them,
As ourselves.
Food that is health-giving to one,
Often brings disease to another.
There are no general set of rules — man made —
For the evolution of mind, soul and body
For all men.
Each must learn to know his own particular force
Of character.
Polarize it,
To time, condition, and locality.
Then can there be no difficulty
In building the Temple.

A man who has the truth
Needs no waste of words to express it.
But he who has no understanding
Must adopt the subterfuge of words
To hold attention, for results expected
That never arrive.

Did you paint your picture of life with regret and failure?
You did this with the best brush and paint you had?
Why not forget your mistake,
And see how easy it is to find a better brush,
And more permanent, slow-drying oil,
So you may correct mistakes,
Or change the color before it hardens
As you did the last picture overnight, because
You thought you might lose the scenery?

If you don't appreciate fine weather as much as you condemn bad
weather; if you don't praise good as much as you criticize bad, you are
lopsided in your judgment and convict yourself accordingly.

Remember a full stomach today will not satisfy you tomorrow.
This morning's opinions will change by tonight.
Expect your compensation in all you do,
Or your journey will be in vain.
All things here are momentary.
You must catch them on the fly as they pass by.
Tomorrow is unborn.
Today is yours.
Yesterday, the skeleton of your efforts made.

No man need envy another.
Nature has so constructed its laws
That each man may create and live in a world of his own;
And as with the stars of heaven,
Need injure none by contact, though living in one mansion.

If all things go wrong do just a little analyzing and find out what you
are thinking with. See if it is the same material with which you thought
when all seemed so bright and happy.

It is not what you think you can do that is convincing, It is what you
already have done, that entitles you to live in the ranks of the
Immortals.

It is not always the brave
Who can exhibit a lot of scars.
Even a careless fool can do that.
But brave men and women have scars deep and livid,
Unseen, deep within their hearts,
And still carry a smile of understanding
With that great character that lives long
After they have passed on.
There are many such people all around you,
Revealed only when catastrophe hovers,
And when real charity and mercy are most in demand,
Then Washingtons and Lincolns are born.

Try to make it difficult to attain what you want
And not only will you be more appreciative and happy,
But permanently contented with your efforts

To just keep warm and comfortable, while others
Are burning up with success or freezing with failure.

When your longings are acute,
You either have something
To give away
Or, something to be filled.
You are either overfed,
Or starving.
You may be rich, yet poor.
Or poor, but wealthy.
Or a poor rich man.

Never climb a mountain that reaches nowhere
And which is more difficult to descend
Than ascend.
The reward of curiosity
Is but to forfeit energy
That might have furthered happiness
And brought joy.
If you have no interest in life,
Reserve your smallest strength
In silence, solitude and rest,
And there will be revealed to you
Your work,
That thoughtlessness and wrong environment
Hid from you.
There is nothing on earth that has life
That does not strive to enlarge,
Beautify, and perpetuate itself
Through desire, vanity and love.

A chosen shepherd should,
And must know of the wolves' habits
As much as what is for the welfare
Of his sheep.
Only then is he a good shepherd.

There is greater virtue in charity shown by the poor than rich, because
of the effort made to relieve distress in the presence of want.

Men may organize the strongest fraternity in the world,
Still Destiny's "fate" orders an individual accounting of each official.
None are exempt from judgement, penalty or reward.
As long as someone shall exceed him,
Facts shall be made known, good or evil, gain or loss.
For when we go to our long sleep,
Everything of material value will be emptied from
The pockets we have worn;
Cash or bonds, worthless or of great value.
So why not do something that will last,
Without regret in the barter of brains and willpower,
So there can be no loss or sorrow
For having done just that thing
That will outlast your name.
Is it so great to have been,
To have had, but not held?
A common thief can steal and hold the scepter of a king.
So hold only that which is becoming and profitable.
It can be done!

He who strives for Truth,
Though he be ever so great a liar,
Will some time shed his coat
And marvel at his own cleanliness.
No one can strive for an Ideal
Unless God has already planted the seed.
One's ideals advertise one's possibilities.
Be a man, or woman, ever so bad,
There is someone who will recognize
Manhood in him
And an Angel in her.

Don't ever try to force intuition, if you expect the truth. You can only be impressed by it. You cannot influence or govern it for it comes to you only according to your worthiness, and your ability to receive it.

If we wish to make a masterpiece we must have the concept in mind first and then materialize it. If we use the hardest marble, the best tools, the work will endure though the labor be strenuous. Under the law of compensation it will pay. So with thought! It is only by deep thinking that we crystalize monuments of endeavors. If we govern

181

thought it means all desires granted. Should we realize that attention and concentration upon a given desire will bring the result, discord and sorrow will be lessened.

But always, must we think our own thoughts, and not those of another. For it is by our own individual thought that we evolve toward perfection. It is not by the thoughts of others. They come to us as echoes, which do record in the Soul's memory as our own.

They are reflections, moon-beams, light that passes us by,
And is reflected back to us.
Thoughts are things that record within the Soul
As sound upon the record of a victrola.
They are echoes of vibration.
They are irritants to the Soul, as light is to the optic nerve,
Sound to the inner ear.

How many people really know how to think?
I see most minds become stimulated by emotion—
By objects the eye sees, by feelings of pain, loss or possession.
Few men give thought full sway.
Few broaden out and allow higher influences
To stimulate their actions.
Few think to make room for new thoughts, new ideas, and things...
It is not so much what a man thinks, as how he thinks
And what he is capable of thinking.
Watch a crowd.
Observe the expression on the faces of the people, their actions.
And you will know what thoughts animate them.
You will also know whence they came, and whither they are going.

I have found that we are not tested
For the day only.
The real test comes in years alone.
We pray in the morning
And expect our reward at night,
While the prayer has not yet reached the ceiling
Of our dwelling.
The seed of prayer lives eternally,
And is not governed by seconds.
Often when we pray for something

And the prayer is barely strong
Enough to stand alone,
It will be carried in the arms
Of an Angel to the Master.
And when the creator of this prayer
Has lived his mortal life,
And passes away,
An answer to his prayer
Will be delivered to his children
After his death
As a recognition from God.

No matter how great or important
Is your work,
Be not blind to the smallest things.
For without them, nothing great
Is permanent.
It is the fibers that hold
Together the strongest oak,
Where then is strength?

He who builds a world of his own
Need never leave it for pleasure.
For the entire world outside
Will try to enter
To keep him company.

It is better to master the language of your own efficiency, so you may
the better recognize and read your own milestones, than to lose time
in deciphering those of your neighbor whose identity lies far from
your own.

There are those who must dig and find gold,
Those who cast and shape it,
And those who chase and engrave it for others to wear
Thus also must there be Thinkers
Who are inspired to find ideas,
For others to write them,
And still others to express them
For others to use and become happy in the possession of.

Many a man would accomplish more in life
If he did not wait
For the approval or flattery of friends.
For when they stop,
Efforts do likewise.
Better that he compete with himself,
As he would in playing solitaire.

A man who excuses
Or defends a lie
Tells two of them.
He who preaches
And does not live it,
Preaches falsely,
No matter what his sermon may be.
He who sets a pace
Must keep it up.
Or he will be crushed by those behind
Who are kept pacing.

Often your thoughts, like your muscles, become tired. Change them,
and you will find complete rest and rejuvenation.

Don't be a too self-confident, arrogant student in your classroom.
Remember that he who gave birth to your lessons
Had to earn his discoveries by hard labor,
Sacrifices, and acknowledgments.
So don't glory in your education
At the price of the humiliation of one
Who has not your opportunities to learn in contented,
Ideal surroundings.
You may have to test and prove your findings
In the place where they were born.

Anger may generate courage.
It may also leave cruelty in its place.
Ambition and desire are fire under a steam boiler,
Powder in a rifle,
Without which there can be no successful purpose.

The noblest thoughts and achievements
Are those created when the human heart works in unison
With its Creator.

He who is wise has a right to judge,
But will not.
He who is ignorant has no right
But does, unwisely.
Therefore, why judge?
It is but to admit or betray
Shortcomings or vices.

One often arrives at a blank wall
Dismayed.
And failing to look up,
One does not see the ladder hanging from on high.

What is worth possessing
Is worth waiting for, and what
Is worth waiting for, is worth possessing.
There is no value to that which has been
Lightly acquired.
It does not represent labor, or even patience,
Hope or love.
Love exists upon love
And willingly carries labor upon its shoulders.

We who would succeed and be happy,
Must first understand discipline,
And live under its rule.

By trying to deceive and fool others,
You are but fooling yourself,
Depriving yourself of the very thing
You are trying to attain.
When you forget how to laugh or play,
It is a sign of danger,
And that the safe cache in the wilderness is being despoiled
Which you must depend upon for sustenance and life
On your way back to complete your life's cycle.
So don't be foolish and deceived,

By gazing into the mirror of your friend's opinion.
Look straight at real life.
Truth is so simple
That children play with it every day
While old men seek it in vain.

No matter how wise your teacher may be,
Remember you use the same tools he does to draw your conclusions.
Your ink of reason may not be so indelible
But if you believe yourself a little more,
Your logic will be self-evident enough not to cheat you,
Or lead you astray.
God, through Nature, has seen to that when
He gave you your mental equipment.

Nature is firmly rooted.
Man can change and travel, tuning himself in to his own.
Why do you laugh at things humorous,
Mostly when tuned in with association, as in a theater?
Seek that which is a feast to your vision
Not too much, or you lose perspective.
Not too little, or it does not appease your appetite.

Anyone without exercise soon dies of idleness,
As a crippled wolf in the wilderness.
Give your ears exercise by hearing good music
And see what mental shape you are in to appreciate it.
See if you can hear the call of your soul and heart
A few words of praise and love,
A command, an inspiration, or your execution.
Give your eyes a little exercise, to see if they recognize landmarks,
Or whether you are lost, and if not,
To see the right from the wrong,
A coming storm, or a friend from a foe.
Give your taste exercise to see if you are eating right food,
Pure air, and fragrance.
See if you can sense the soul of the earth
And its flowers by their aroma.
Do these things, and you soon will be active,
Eliminating or absorbing, to give out the fruits
That only such a masterpiece as your body can achieve.

To the betterment of everything that has life,
To prove your own activity, which alone can be life.

Truth is so simple
That children play with it every day
While old men seek it in vain.

Why desecrate this hour of day by fear of disaster;
When that day and hour has already been set?
For even death requires but a moment:
But see how many hours of torture you have made it
And still are yet to die.

Have you ever analyzed what you really wanted,
And then acquired it, only to find
That you did not need it,
Could not afford it
And could do without it without sacrifices,
Save when possessing it, in keeping it?
How many wants are there to want
But never to possess?
Once in your keeping, you are more unhappy
Than when still wanting them.

What is it to be happy and contented? Is it to look forward to
something? To labor to put away for a rainy day that never comes? To
hoard until there is enough for a cloud to drown your children?

Much is hidden from those who will not seek.
I often test my friends.
If a grain of truth dropped,
Fails to grow,
I do not repeat the experiment.
It is useless to try to grow certain plants out of season.

We stumble
And knock down the domino ahead of us.
Which knocks down the next ahead,
And that the next,
And so on, till out of sight.
And we soon forget the blunder made,

Until we are awakened
By a blow from behind,
Which knocks us down,
And discloses the fact
That the dominoes of life
Are arranged in circles.
If we hit one ahead,
We must expect,
Sooner or later,
The blow from behind.

If you think that you have discovered
New Truths,
Do not be in haste
To disclose them.
They will not vanish.
They will grow.
Keep the roots,
And give away the fruit only.

He who prays
Is benefitted more by praying
Than in having his prayer answered.

What picture shall we set in the frame of the mind today?
It is for each one to choose.
Shall it be the picture of yesterday's mistake unfinished,
Or just a new background of tomorrow's masterpiece?
Each mortal has a garden,
An individual responsibility.
You have no right to work in your neighbor's garden,
And so neglect your own.
Neither have you a right to expect
Your neighbor to work in yours,
And influence him to neglect his own.
For all gardens of love hold love, hold loveliness,
Whatever we sow, will grow.

Never seek an inspiration,
Or think of one,
Unless you intend to write it,

Or record it in action of some form.
If you disregard an inspiration
When it is given you,
Then will it disregard you
When you seek it.

If you look at a man and like him
He must be good if you are good.
Your best judgement is your highest standard
Of your individual education.

The future is for you to will and shape.
The present is concrete.
Past, it is gone forever.

Your strength in the chain of life is but the strength of its weakest
link. So test each link before you weld yourself to others, or your
reserve strength will be superfluous while the weaker feels safe.

The motion of the mind is thought.
And anything whatsoever that gives rise to thought is life-giving.
We all must admit that "as we think, so we are."
We make ourselves what we are by how we think.
If we are not what we want to be, it is our own fault
In wrong thinking...
A beautiful green meadow covers the unsightly earth
Of dead resolutions.
Each blade of grass is a monument to the masses.
Each flower reaching into the air is a monument to the genius,
The martyr, the man or the woman who dares carry out
The aspiration of their souls.

Be happy in the thought that all your possibilities and blessings thus
far have not unfolded themselves. You still have before you a
realization beyond your present comprehension. It is impossible for
you to draw a picture which you have not seen unless you make it a
composite, using that which is already in memory. But it requires new
actual experiences, and new emotions and new designs which you
require from environments, to make you realize greater sensations and
joys.

Many times we forget to remember,
But when the waters have been troubled
Let us remember to forget.

Man seldom breaks through the walls
Of his Infancy.
But when he does, he becomes a Philosopher.
And he sees not the inside of the egg
In which he was born.
But the limitless space
And Eternity.

You know we often think ourselves misunderstood, when we ourselves who misunderstand others. It is best that we live on the borderline of pain and sorrow that we may the better realize our duty and our mission. And that may be constantly awake to danger. We must ever avoid too much pain, or we shall become callous and heedless of the warning when the limitations of one of Nature's laws has been reached. Indeed, that is what pain is, such a warning.

Measure your success not by the competitors you have beaten, But by the new friends that have come to make your acquaintance.

It is not always the sins we have committed that call us to account at our maturity; but the virtues we have neglected that demand an uneasy conscience.

Labor, discipline and self-control still the fire of impulse, so the hand of virtue may lead on to fill the void created by environments contrary to the growth of enlightenment.

The big "sins" we need not fear.
We see them and guard against them.
It is the little germs,
The little seeds and first thoughts
That are unseen
But scattered everywhere
That deserve our greatest attention.

You can only prove friendship by deeds and sacrifices
Not charity and gifts,
But understanding and loyalty.

Learn the meaning of the word, "Appreciation,"
And half of your faults, sins and disappointments
Will have vanished.

Do you think it an honor
To have brought up a child
As much as a child
To have given a parent
An opportunity to have brought up a child
By the discipline of Personal Responsibility?
So that after all, the score is even,
As fatherhood and childhood.

If you wish to avoid sorrow, then eat and drink of life's joys moderately. Reserve the surplus for the time when you will be hungry and thirsty. Your greatest blessing, misused, can become your greatest curse.

Time your efforts to Success by the clock of Nature. If you wish to live but for a day of splendor, then time yourself by seconds. But if you wish to bloom eternally, then count your efforts by centuries.

Great men forget great things done,
But will weep because they failed to accomplish
What a child is capable of doing.

There are sorrows which time alone can cure
By what light we find appertaining to Eternity.
When we deliberately close one eyelid, we do not destroy the light,
But only shut it from our own view.
That light which but reflects itself, lends its truth,
Brings out the soul of that which it touches.
So keep your eyes open.
At best they see but dimly.

It is the sculptor who hews the hardest stone,
The writer who uses the most permanent ink,

And the philosopher the most simple truths,
Who rides the tempests and survives the dark ages of time...

As we think and act, so are we.
Our thoughts leave an indelible mark upon our features,
While our actions leave monuments
In the graveyards of the memories of others.

An intelligent man fears an ignorant man
Because of that ignorant man's ignorance.
An ignorant man fears an intelligent man
Because of that knowledge the intelligent man
Possesses is unknown to the ignorant.
The suspicions of the ignorant create fear that weakens.
The intelligent man is aware of that weakness,
So is strengthened.

Which plant or bulb in the human garden
Do you water and cultivate most?
What blossoms are most pleasing to you?
Cultivate all,
Until each blooms
To your own satisfaction;
And then you will KNOW
What constitutes your creation.

If you assume the adoption of a child, be sure that you do your duty
as a parent, and it may be a better child to you than your own, and
even teach you how to be a good father or mother.

Obey the simple things of life
And the big things will not overthrow you.
Choose the correct grains of sand,
And the house of bricks will not crumble.
Likewise with an army.

We have been given just so much energy, like money,
To spend as we will, or throw away.
What shall we do with it?

To believe in a God
Is the most perfect principle
To attain perfection.
To imitate a God,
The quickest way to attain that which we seek.
For it is the wish itself
Clothed in reality
Which but strives to manifest itself
Through Faith,
In its own individuality.

I believe that some men
Have been made leaders
And have been given great missions to perform
For Humanity.
And it is far better to give to the man
One pound of sugar
So that he may be better able
To carry out the great work
Than to give to hundreds and thousands
Human beings,
One grain each,
And have all lost.

We are all too close to our labor and acquaintances
To see truthfully as things really are.
Just widen the space and see for yourself.

If your education does not give you contentment,
Happiness, confidence, and success,
You have been cheated.
And that by yourself.

Life and history repeat themselves constantly.
Go count your cycles, that you may improve, and profit by mistakes.

A fool, on meeting a Philosopher
Will, with arrogance say,
"There goes a fool."
But the Philosopher smiles sorrowfully,

With pity, and answers with humility:
"Thou hast said it."

There is a first seemingly, insignificant step
Unseen,
Unknown;
Which leads to Heaven or Hell.
It is at the point,
Where temptation has no string,
Where life and death are synonymous.
It is at the point
Where we may turn future tears
Into future smiles.
It is at the point
Beyond which we are conditioned.
Beyond which — as we say,
We are in the hands of "Fate".

He who is wise but humble invites love and respect where a fool has
contempt and invites it.

The real wise man has sought all he knows from within himself; the
intellectual man from others.

Man loses sight
Of that stupendous law of Progress.
He thinks Progress will not go on,
Without his egotistical activity;
And is startled into realization
Only when he sees himself engulfed
And strangled by the achievements
Of the younger generation,
Which ever settle about Old Age.

Measure your sanity
By how long your imagination
Can remain within the walls
Of common sense and reason.

He who will not be hungry
Cannot enjoy an appetite.

He who does not love
Cannot receive.
The only way to receive is to give.
He who gives, cleanses himself.
He who only takes, decays.
An empty room contains
The most fresh air.
A vacant nest has fulfilled
The purpose of Nature.
He who would be successful and happy
Let him do the labor he can do best,
And in his own way.
His individuality will place him
In his own sphere.
For we are all labeled, classified, ordained.
Or there would be no beginning,
Nor end,
Nor birth, nor death, in this life.
We all represent the symbol of time.
If you would gain knowledge
And be wise,
Learn from the tongues of babes and fools.
Instead of your wise men,
Who may know the sun's eclipses
Years in advance;
The distance of the stars,
And the name of every insect;
And who, in themselves are not happy,
And do not know love's companionship.
A child will teach you your needs.
A fool, what to avoid.

It is easier to prevent a bruise than to heal one. Easier to prevent and control habits by education, than to cure them.

If you will remember the following it may solve
Some of your problems:
Does not today's food feed tomorrow's ambition?
Then why do you insist upon adding adulteration and flavors
To strangle your own special make of bread,
So that the owner of your borrowed flavor but claims his own,

As well as yours, to his credit.
Feed tomorrow's thought with your ambitions
And ideals of yesterday;
For those ideals are just what you are,
And may become what you long for most.
They are your choice of food when hungry, if you only know it.
Man's taste has been so abused, his desires so misshaped,
That he orders a big meal which is served too soon, or too late,
His unnatural desires having so much sway
That there is no coordination in his entire system
Then he bemoans his fate until Nature slows him down by force.
Be normal in all things;
For the deeper you sink in the ground the more labor,
And the less you find but materialism.
The higher you fly, the more mysterious clouds
Of spiritual fanaticism.
Still, both may produce a supermind.
But the happiest of the three is he who insists
On walking on the surface of the earth,
With feet among the flowers, heart and head overlooking
Beauty and happiness.

You are ready to condemn the man who has made a mistake —
Is it because you envy,
But dare not make the same mistake
For want of an opportunity?
If not, where is your charity and tolerance, pity, and pride
For being stronger?

A fool can ask a question that a wise man cannot answer.
And if he could, the fool would not understand it.

The strong arm of the sculptor brings into existence the artist's greatest
inspiration in the hardest marble. His masterpiece may then be lasting,
and remembered and loved by future generations. Do you not think it
is a law that he who is most valued must be visited by tragedies, tests
of endurance, humiliation and sorrow?

Where is your quest?
Do you intend to rush heedlessly over numerous paths and by-paths,

Or will you remain in your own Soul poised and well-balanced?
You may have a light buggy in which you are going to
Ride around the world.
Are you not going to sit in the exact center of that buggy,
Realizing that the four wheels will carry you safely back home?
If you were to sit above one of the wheels only,
It surely would be worn out before the other three.
And your mission would not be fulfilled.
Your quest would be in vain.
Common sense is in using every faculty of the brain.
Not riding to a judgment on one wheel...
Remain in the center of your Soul, where there is an answer
To your quest.

It is not enough to possess power;
It is more essential
To know how to use it.
Do not envy one
Who displays it unwisely,
For he soon
Will be dispossessed of it,
As with one
Who possesses wealth unguarded.

A heart of gold has its many temptations --
More so than the heart of stone.

THERE ONCE WAS A MAN
Who was born in the depths of the valley of Nothingness.
He beheld the wonderful Sun in the heavens
That seemed to give life to all living things.
He made himself a vehicle, with a strong pair of tugs.
He loaded it with provisions and started up a mountain
To be nearer this life-giving thing.
But the climb was difficult—a continuous pull on the tugs.
Every once in a while he came across the mistakes of others
Who like him endeavored to reach the top,
But would slip and spill their load.
They would implore him to help them,
In exchange for some of their goods.
And in the doing of this charity, his muscles became hard as steel;

Until at last he had reached the top, to behold the splendor at his feet.
But as he turned about, he was astonished
To behold a deep valley at his feet and a great mountain before him.
For he had but reached the top of a little foothill,
Called his mortal life.
Still he remained for a time, bathing himself
In the glory of his achievements
Until at last the sun went down.
Then the greatest Ambition was born — to climb the real mountain.
Still, how could he descend into the valley, and ascend the next?
For he realized that this side of the foothill mountain
Was as smooth as glass,
Where no one could ascend; nor once descended,
Could one stop his flight,
Because this was the valley of death.
Here his physical strength did him naught.
Still, realizing that the great load he had pulled up
To the top would be capitalized with his momentum,
He prepared to descend.
By the help of his own deeds, and with the swiftness of light
Was carried down through oblivion.
And by the momentum was carried up to the great
Mountain of Compensation,
To the exact height of the foothill he had just left.
And there he stood, firm under foot,
And his passage paid for by his deeds and wisdom thus far adopted
And now he possessed a continued want,
Which is the greatest blessing on earth.
It is the pull of the compass, a definite fact,
The direct road to that place where intense activity
Become calm and peaceful.

Nature gives birth to nothing to which it does not give
Sustenance to exist,
And protection for a given time,
Of which to make use according to the understanding
Created by experience.
The human body is the fertile ground
In which the roots of the soul make themselves known,
And as with the little colored flag of the plant, the blossom,

Introducing an individuality, and the coming of the fruit --
So it is with men and women.

What is pain
If not but a faithful voice of warning
Of disobedience to the laws of Nature
Under which we exist?

A cruel man uses anger
To avenge his cowardly blindness.
Bear in mind that often, if you don't do,
You can't.

Have you ever observed
How the needle of a phonograph travels,
Touching every point of the record?
Why don't you do likewise,
With the opportunities of your territory,
Which is your record?
Why just keep in one depression,
Repeating over and over yesterday's activity,
Leaving out all the rest of your life's songs;
Then complain of its briefness,
Until someone else begins where you left off,
Only to place the flowers on your coffin
Because of songs unsung?
Wake up and sing them now.
Adjust the needle out of the same rut habit
And let the world know that God makes no mistake,
But that it is man only, who forgets
That which masters try to remind him of.
Is it not true ?

One must concentrate upon his purpose,
Be it what it may,
Or make his mind receptive to inspiration upon
A chosen subject only,
Or he may receive thoughts not essential,
But detrimental to his development.

Grief and calamity are two of the finest whips
To bring us joy and success.

Every man is forced to exist or die. Then why not make your choice
where you will live best; for contentment, not momentary pleasure
with sorrow, despair and regrets? One can choose his own flower pot
to grow in, after leaving nature's great Hot-house: even to choosing
those who may admire you and love you for just what you are.

I dare not tell you of what is really ahead of you. If you knew you
would stretch out your arms toward the blue sky with tears in your
eyes, and a longing in your heart to fly, to soar upward because of the
distant beauty that is yours. I have glimpsed that land of beauty. And
have been enamored by its magic. But at times I dare not linger there,
for fear of neglecting objectiveness.

If you do not labor for a purpose, you place no value on it.
For a thing, no matter how precious, is of no value unless you
Place there yourself by what you would do to obtain it.
If you find and win the love of a woman, with but little effort,
You will lose her to another, as easily as you won her.
But if it required half a lifetime, as in climbing
A mountain to its height,
You will know the journey down, though more pleasant,
Has as many miles of road as going up.
So measure your value by what is required to obtain it.

Never profess to do more than you can.
The effort to maintain your assertion
Will be greater than the reward
From your deception.
With the same amount of energy
You could do better things
In your own way
The things that are yours to do.

When disputing over an opinion
Why not give your own
To match that of your opponent,
Rather than to produce none,
And only destroy his.

Why not give something in return
As a friendly bargain,
Instead of giving birth
To disappointed enemies.

You say you were never lost? But have you shown the way to others?
If not, then you ARE lost.

How could we exist,
Were it not for a purpose?
If we do not know that purpose
It should be our purpose to seek it,
Slowly but surely.

Every man when lost
Must find himself
Or he will dispute
That he was ever lost
If someone else
Points out the right road.

Before considering being converted or initiated,
Do not accept the laws blindly.
You may buy that which you cannot support;
Obligate yourself to that which you cannot fulfill,
Breaking a law assumed without the sanction of your
Willingness and understanding,
Changing your entire makeup to obey the law of another;
Sinning for having broken a promise,
Assuming a law which will affect even your conscience,
Because that law seems to be an inspiration
Until you once find yourself in mental nakedness
Then you will become its enemy
Instead of a tolerant human being.
Always be convinced logically and practically,
So there will be no residue of a soap bubble left to shame you.
How many martyrs have died in the past,
Convinced they died for a sacred Cause.
But we today call them fanatics, spies, traitors,
Revolutionists, "ahead of their times,"
But nevertheless they were truly martyrs

Worthy of a crown and of their convictions.
Be sure your heart is with your mind,
Before you accept in haste
Anything that you intend to graft on your tree of life,
So when it bears fruit,
That branch will not hold fruit that will shame your own;
Though your own may be lemons (so essential to life),
And your adopted branch peaches
God made nothing useless
Not even the tail of a pig.

Nature has created our understanding
As the embryo of a chick,
Within an opaque shell.
So it might not, in its development
And involuntary growth,
Desire those things
Outside its own world.
This shell is opaque and brittle,
Until, by wisdom and knowing,
It becomes transparent.
Then knowledge removes
The superstitious potash, --
Brittleness, --
And makes it transparent,
And flexible, — to shape itself
According to its will and emotions.
Thus it is with ourselves.
As we evolve from ignorance and rigidity
Were we to see into the beyond,
We could not carry out the creation
Of our primitive worlds.
As we grow,
We tear away the veils,
Shaping ourselves according to the niche
We are destined to fill.
And only by degrees do we become aware
Of why our creation.
The purpose of all things we question.
But the Great Architect
Has placed life's answer

In every loving form.
And we could if we would,
Read the messages from the Father
To His self-Creating Sons.

Some men become famously wealthy,
Insisting on being in debt.

The scrubbing brush to a working woman
Is as important as the pen
To the President of the United States.
Never ridicule the flimsy bridge
You have just passed over.
You may have to use it
On your return trip.

If environments cannot be altered, it is well to have a few apparent
calamities so that under the law of relativity, one is made to give more
value to that which has become commonplace by familiarity.

The greatest sorrow and tragedy in life
Comes to those who seek happiness at the end of the trail
Rather than in the making of the trail.

If you wish to hold
What you think is yours,
Be sure that it is paid for.
And by your own coin.
Remembering, incidentally,
That each penny represents its value in deeds.
Or your possession is but a debt.

If you interest yourself in the roots of a rose,
The blossom will be interested in you.

He who wins friends by frankness
Holds them without flattery.

If personality is good salesmanship,
Then the salesman
Must have sold himself the facts

Enough to believe them absolutely
To convince the buyer of the facts.
Then why not convince teachers and missionaries
To convince themselves first,
Before trying to convince others
Of that which they themselves have certain doubts
At least enough so to be sold by those
Who do believe, even though they may be mistaken.
At least there will be some
Who will be entirely convinced of facts
By the mistakes made by him
Who did believe, and still was mistaken.
Be sure you outlive your apprenticeship
Before assuming mastership
Or some pupil
May hail you as an equal
To your embarrassment among masters.

Always be yourself.
Then you'll know what you are,
And what you can be.

If you wish the world to follow you,
Keep on walking alone without looking back.
And when you have reached your goal
A multitude will be at your back.

Miracles are not so convincing as the fruits of them.
Christ did not convince the leaders of His time,
But the fruits of His work convinced the world.

Prevent rather than cure
By studying not only that which you're thinking with
But the material you have with which to shape
That which does your thinking.
For your state of mind can be what you will it to be
By the right purpose in willing.

Learn how to forget what you should, or will,
As well as to remember that which again may be

Born to you beneficially,
So as to correct that mistake you ought to forget in its correction.

When you ridicule another,
You have been blinded by the same vice in a new form
As that of which you accuse your victim.
Just as he fails to understand his own knowledge of wisdom,
Or he whose physical strength makes him arrogant
Only to be humiliated by one who may be weak but not aware of it.

How many people fear to lose their good living
By leaving their hypocrisy behind?
Who advocates truth so that nobody may question his sincerity
Nor expose him to ridicule because of lack of truth?

Our bad habits make us prisoners,
And our false pride is the jailer that keeps us there.

You are what you are; but can be what you will.

We always lose sight of what we've got, in our efforts to obtain what
we haven't got.

When adversity comes, it is a sign that we are given a test, or given
work to do. The Masters test only those whom they feel to be
worthwhile, so as to be sure of results.

If you have found some truth,
Don't get over-excited and brag about it,
Or you may be checked up
To prove how ignorant you have been.
Rather add it to your stock of knowledge
For it is then already accepted,
And your word is law,
For that is truth.

Thoughts are bound to escape that may be injurious,
Your tongue of ill-reproof is evidence of that.
Think twice, for and against,
Before you think of thoughts you intend to express.

Do well, and conquer your work,
However menial,
And you will have done
What Christ did,
When He died upon the Cross.
And for the same purpose.

Sit down and meditate: from within, a new world shall be born, in place of what you are forced to accept.

If you lose yourself in serving men, God will find you to be served.

If you can't think it out, you can't act it out.

Each Individual must keep his balance if he wishes to succeed and be happy, and be always under some good discipline to adopt a personal mental control governed by logic, reason and justice.

When the time comes that the public may know and realize what supposedly great men think about instead of what they talk about, you will behold a welcome miracle in the adjustment of man-made laws as influenced by God-made laws.

Don't think for a moment
That you can always get away
With those things that you try to prevent others getting away with.

Misfortune only follows when we starve our intuition,
Or follow the dictates of another into slavery.

A person who does not improve things is not improving himself.

Did you ever try to change your mind when angry?
Try it, and see what you are made of.
Don't lock up your reason when it is needed more.
When you start in to lick a man,
Notice if it is the same man you hit with your first blow.

As you climb the mountain to success, be sure to look down periodically, as you do upward. It will make you more cautious and

sure of your worthiness. It will show you from what rank you came,
and to what depths you may fall.

Many a man has been forced to great deeds,
Who capitalizes unearned reward,
While many a worthy martyr died in obscurity
To have his name and deeds resurrected in the selfish
Display of glory
That might have saved him to us in untold wisdom.
Far rather sustain life and receive living food for knowledge
Than only his dead memory of words, with no reply.
The world looks big to little men.
The world is small to big men.

Many an educated man becomes a fool through a leaky tongue.
Many an ocean liner sinks by a slow leak because
Too insignificant to notice such magnitude.
Still, a drop of kerosene in five gallons of milk manifests itself.
Let him who is always so ready to dispute the things of the spirit
Deny the existence of the evaporated brandy that he
Ran through his leaky still,
And when evaporated into the air
Ask him where it is.
Or have him color a glass full of alcohol;
And later when he finds the glass empty,
And only the color remaining,
Ask him where it is
And if it is not a fact that had he placed his glass
Full of alcohol in an air-tight room,
He would have found it condensed on the floor,
To prove that the thing he could not see after it left the glass,
Was still there.
Likewise with spiritual things.

It is better and safer to shape and build your cocoon
With own hands and material,
Instead of borrowing from your thoughtless neighbor
Who not only needs his own material but gives you
What is unfit for your protection —
Providing you expect the wings to carry you from
The blossom of achievements to the fruits of understanding.

Because you think you have no chance to make good,
Don't give up;
For who told you that anyone was better than you are
If you did not make comparison
With someone you thought greater than you?
Why not let them
Really compare their achievements with yours
And see where you stand?
And then, if they were in your place,
Where really is the goal
That you both are traveling for?
Just wait until you both get inside
Of the bright lights of the City,
And let's see the paces of both of you.
That is the time you make your speed.
And there are more country miles than city miles.
So come on and "click."

Forget past failures by remembering future possibilities.

We are just what we are
And can make ourselves what we intend to
If our intentions are sincere.
A man without a want
Is a ship without a rudder or compass.
And a man with a real want
Has already sensed
The laurel leaves of Victory;
Has already inhaled the fragrant rose
Of the seed he is about to plant.
And if I am able to do this,
Then every human being is able to do likewise
For we are all constituted alike.
We all possess the seven prismatic colors with which to paint
Nature.
We all possess the seven notes of music
So that we may sing and hear.
We all live through the seven epochs of
Seven years each of life.
And we labor six days in the week, to rest
Upon the seventh.

And we sit outdoors after a terrific storm
To behold the rainbow of seven colors
That tries to teach us of its message
Which was created for man and woman alone.
How futile it would be for an artist to create
A masterpiece with a primary color lacking;
For a musician to interpret life
With only three notes.
And it is thus with those who have failed.
They have failed to find
And make use of the seven opportunities
Which they possess.

Intuitive people think the same thoughts. It is neither coincidence nor telepathy when two radios, attuned to the same broadcast, play the same tune.

We have no right to starve our emotions.
We have need of them all
If only to counteract certain resultant evils.
But if you would succeed as you should
Be sure to hire a caretaker
For each emotion that manifests itself
Above normal.

Most people seldom drink from their own springs of Inspiration.
They drink from their neighbor's stagnant pool of waste,
Allowing their own spring of running water
The water of life — to dry up.
Our own spring of water
Will flow only when we use the water
And when the mouth of the spring is kept clean
And clear of debris.
By wrong thinking we merely exist.
By right thinking we drink of the pure waters of life.

When a good soldier kneels to pray
Before the battle,
He does not expect God's legions
To fight his battle.
He expects to be inspired

By the sense of justice
And then, himself, to do the fighting
That is required of him.

It is well to endure a little sorrow, to give birth to pity, sympathy, mercy, charity and love.

Sit down and meditate; from within, a new world shall be born — in place of what you have been forced to accept.

I would rather make keys to unlock doors
Than locks to lock them.
The man who locks up riches is in danger of losses always.
He who makes keys can look forward to profits.
He encourages production, honesty, circulation and progress.
The man who locks up riches, does so only for self-gratification,
Which encourages men to become dishonest,
Covetous, selfish and criminal.
If we think we have the most perfect metal,
Or organization, and hoard it up,
How can there be improvements?
If preventive measures are used, why not encourage
Even the beggar to give up his mental secrets to mankind,
Instead of making a criminal of him by discouragement.
Give every man a chance, and he will make or break himself,
And not be only a beggar,
But either a man or nothing at all.

Many a child is lost on the broad sea of life by
The mother's selfish love,
Depriving her child of that compass of free action
And search for self-reliance,
That only means wreckage or slavery when that mother
Passes on with that compass — her child's individuality.

Man, in idleness, makes food for his master,
Losing sight of its mission
Which, far from being ornamental,
Is to be a necessity in his activity.

Is it not gratifying to rest?
But how can one enjoy rest if he is not tired?
How become honestly tired without labor?
And why labor without reward?
And how can one accept reward without earning it,
When it must he paid for in full?

Try to live so that the unseen world may have more respect for you
than those who flatter you, in order to forget your virtues and make
you forget their sins.

If indeed the sparrow's fall is recorded
Then the prayer of a child of God
Will surely reach on High
And be answered,
Even though the answer comes
At the pace of a snail.

It is the green lithe limb that bends before the wind of adversity.
When the proud, stiff limb refuses, and is torn off.

When I go into a church, I make-believe the Master is there.
And then I don't ask him for anything.
I thank him for what I have.

Are things worthwhile?
Then make yourself a part of those things
With which you wish to be identified.
And they cannot exist with you.

Condemnation, ridicule and envy are always made use of
In trying to prevent a real man from climbing the ladder of success.

It is often your superfluous energy that gets you into trouble:
Your extra money to gamble, into problems.
So make good use of it by controlling the impulse of
Extravagance, waste, and mere chance.

It is as we cast our bread upon the waters
That counts,
And not the returns we expect to get.

We are paid for each kind act or deed,
The gold is at the end of the rainbow.
But think not at all of the earnings,
Beware of spiritual greed.
And in a mad race let us not dissipate
Our strength indiscreetly
And be prevented from furthering the greater work.
Some are called to be sheep,
Some are called to be shepherds,
Some hunger—others feed.
But though we are asked for bread,
We must also eat and drink
That our strength may sustain us
To fulfil the law of evolution
And that we may tread the road
Leading to Eternity.
And then will the rainbow
Be a halo about the head
Of a Child of God.

213